Loss and Grief in Medicine

Peter W. Speck, M.A., B.Sc.
Hospital Chaplain, Northern General Hospital
Sheffield Area Health Authority (Teaching)

BAILLIERE TINDALL·LONDON

A BAILLIÈRE TINDALL book published by
Cassell Ltd,
35 Red Lion Square, London WC1R 4SG
and at Sydney, Auckland, Toronto, Johannesburg
an affiliate of Macmillan Publishing Co. Inc.
New York

First published 1978

ISBN 0 7020 0681 5

Printed in Great Britain by Thomson Litho Ltd, East Kilbride

British Library Cataloguing in Publication Data

Speck, Peter W
    Loss and grief in medicine.
    1. Hospital patients—Psychology   2. Grief
    I. Title
    362.1 '0422   RA965.3

ISBN 0–7020–0681–5

Dedication

To my parents
To my wife Elisabeth
and our children, David and Jane,
and all others who have assisted
my growth in understanding
and concern

Contents

Foreword

Loss and Grief in Medicine unfolds and develops a wide understanding of loss and resultant grief in a variety of contexts.

The caring aspects of medicine are not easy to define and needs which are ill-defined embarrass and remain unmet by reason of the lack of definition.

Loss and grief are normal parts of living; anger and frustration are normal parts of grieving; and the work of grief is demonstrated in these chapters.

Teaching student doctors, nurses, social workers and clergy factors associated with clinical states all too easily obliterates the imagination and understanding necessary for total caring. The examples of loss worked through by the author illustrate situations which are common in most general hospitals and the associated community groups. The very personal examples quoted from a wide experience of needs serve the text well.

The inclusion of simple but clear teaching of the cultural and religious influences makes the book a practical reference source as well as performing its primary task of enhancing understanding of the grief caused by handicaps, the grief caused by surgical mutilation and the 'little deaths' which may precede total death leading to wholeness.

This book should contribute to enhance understanding and caring for all who use it.

June, 1978

Valerie Hunt
S.R.N., S.C.M., O.N.D., R.N.T.
District Nursing Officer, Avon Health Authority;
formerly Director of Nurse Education,
Sheffield Area Health Authority

Preface

In recent years there has been an increasing concern with learning how to meet the needs of dying patients and of bereaved people. This has led to a corresponding increase in the number of books and articles which deal with various aspects of death, grief and bereavement. Most of these focus on the reaction of people either to the loss of their own life or the loss of a loved one through death.

When I was asked if I would be willing to contribute to this field of study I was concerned that, with one or two exceptions, very little seemed to have been written about the reactions of people to other forms of loss. In my own experience, as a hospital chaplain, it has become increasingly clear that one can often observe a 'grief like' reaction in people who have experienced the loss of a body part, of a function or of their sense of usefulness. It is out of this experience, and the shared experience of others, that the present book grew.

While not claiming to be a comprehensive text the book examines the wider meaning of the terms *loss* and *grief* and looks at the relevance of these concepts in a medical setting. It is envisaged that the book may prove helpful to nurses, doctors, social workers, clergy and others involved in health care.

The book is in three parts. The first part examines the concepts of loss, grief and anticipatory grieving and support. The second part of the book considers the relevance of these concepts in three areas of health care: obstetrics and gynaecology; general surgery; and general medicine. The final part looks at the influences of culture and religious belief on the reactions of people to their experience of loss.

The discussion topics in Appendix 1 are offered as a means of relating the material in the book to ourselves, both personally and professionally. It is envisaged that such discussions might be interdisciplinary, using examples from our own experience.

June, 1978   Peter W. Speck

Acknowledgements

The experience drawn upon in the writing of this book goes back over many years of hospital and parish life. It is appropriate, therefore, to acknowledge the many patients, families, friends and colleagues, past and present, who have allowed me the privilege of sharing and learning from their experiences of loss and grief.

During the period when I have been preparing this book I have been grateful to various colleagues at the Northern General Hospital, Sheffield, and the community it serves, who have read or discussed the manuscript with me at various stages of development. Their comments, suggestions and criticisms have been most valuable.

It is always difficult to single out particular people, but I wish to thank especially Dr A. J. Anderson and Mrs Rosemary Anderson; Mr Ernest Beer (Principal Social Worker), Mr R. T. Clegg, Mr B. J. Fairbrother, Miss Eileen Mann and Dr B. A. Ridgway.

I am also grateful to Dorothy Berrow, Denise Knighton, Glynis Mallinson, Elaine Johnston and Miss Nancy Philcox for their assistance with typing the manuscript, as well as to Mrs Kate Suggate for the preparation of the index.

Most importantly I must thank Miss Valerie Hunt for writing the foreword to the book.

All quoted sources are acknowledged in the text of the book.

Special acknowledgment is made to the United Feature Syndicate, Inc. for permission to use the Peanuts cartoon.

The two photographs in Chapter 8 are reproduced by permission of the Director of the India Office Library and Records, and permission to reproduce part of an article, *East Comes West*, I wrote about Muslim, Hindu and Sikh patients in 1976 is acknowledged to the *Nursing Times*.

All biblical quotations are from the Revised Standard Version of the Bible and are used by permission of the Division of Christian Education of the National Council of the churches of Christ in the United States of America, and the publishers, William Collins.

Part One
The Concepts of Loss and Grief

Introducing Concepts

A life that was all 'ups' must seem like a Utopia to many who are experiencing a 'down' period in their life. Lucy's desire to avoid the 'downs' is a strong one and a natural one. However, if the 'downs' can be approached in a positive way, with support and guidance from others, they can lead to growth and development in many directions. But this process can often be slow, and at times it may be painful.

The young child who has learnt to stand, holding onto someone's hand, has to totter forward into the unknown for a few steps before reaching the safety of another hand. Inevitably there are falls, but the child looks to the adult for encouragement and rarely shows anxiety, unless it is conveyed by the adult. The child falls repeatedly and picks himself or herself up with determination, encouraged by the adult, and makes the attempt again. The new freedom and success are sufficient reward and the old status of 'crawler' gives way to that of 'toddler'.

This change of status is only one of many that take place during the course of our life and such 'critical events' are a characteristic of the normal growth and development of an individual. The first of these is the process of birth leading to successive stages which include learning to walk and talk, school, puberty, the first job, courtship, marriage, birth of children, illness, death of a relative or friend, advent of old age and retirement, and ultimately one's own death. In addition to such normal crises a person may also experience such events as domestic tragedy, redundancy, injury leading to a permanent disability, or disappointment in love. These events may still lead to growth if the individual can be enabled to work through the emotional disturbance and to develop his character and personality. However, as with all crises the person may regress to an earlier stage of development instead. One of the best known exponents of 'Crisis Theory' is Professor Gerald Caplan who has described a crisis as

Our concept of what happens when a person faces a difficulty, either a threat of loss or a loss, in which his existing coping repertoire is insufficient, and he therefore has no immediate way of handling the stress ... what you get at the end of crisis is a new equilibrium. The new equilibrium, if the psychological work has been satisfactory, results in external adaptation and internal adjustment. If the psychological work has not been satisfactory, there is also a new equilibrium, but this new equilibrium is one of regression.[1]

[1] Caplan (1969) pp. 41 and 43.

Medicine is intimately associated with crisis and members of the caring professions are in contact with people at times when they are facing new and often difficult situations. Frequently these people have had no previous experience of the events they are facing and their perception may be distorted by anxiety. The first response usually is to try to deal with it by trial and error, and if that is not effective the level of anxiety and frustration begins to rise. The person then starts to feel uncomfortable and wishes to escape from the stress-inducing situation. Assistance is needed if the person is to find an appropriate way to act and to use the experience creatively (to 'withstand'[1] it) for personal and interpersonal growth. The direction in which we move will depend upon the support we receive and the results of our previous experiences of crisis and loss. We shall, therefore, look at our understanding of the experience of loss and normal grieving.

References and Further Reading

Caplan, G. (1969) *An Approach to Community Mental Health.* London: Tavistock Publications.

Wilson, M. (1975) *Health is for People.* London: Barton, Longman and Todd.

---

[1] Wilson (1975) p. 75.

1   *The Experience of Loss and Normal Grief*

> They must go free
> Like fishes in the sea
> Or starlings in the skies
> Whilst you remain
> The shore where casually they come again.
>
> Frances Cornford

The letting go of many of our childhood attachments is an important part of our growth to maturity. Such 'letting go' frequently generates feelings of loss to which we have to accommodate. But with the passage of time, we usually find that it is less necessary to keep returning to the 'shore' from which we came and where we felt comfortable and safe, for we have moved towards a greater personal independence.

Our Experience of Loss

From birth to death we experience many losses, whether actual or threatened, and our reaction to them influences the character we develop and the attitudes we form. Birth necessitates being deprived of the security of the womb, and relinquishing the breast for solid food, losing a favourite toy and leaving home for the first time are all forms of loss with which we learn to cope. The various types of loss experienced during our life *can* serve to prepare us to some extent for the ultimate loss—of our own life. Such deprivations may be described as *anticipatory losses*, or 'little deaths'.

The loss may be of an object, a limb, an organ, a person or a relationship, and clearly some losses will represent a much bigger threat to our well-being than others. There seems no reason for believing that all types and degrees of loss will result in similar reactions or an equal awareness of grief for what is past and gone. We may in fact not realize, until after it has occurred, whether a given crisis is to be construed as a loss or a gain. For example, a person who sells his car because he is under financial pressure may perceive it as a loss. However, if he subsequently hears that the new owner has had to spend a lot of money on the car because of unexpected new faults that have developed, he may now be glad the vehicle is not his.

Frequently it is not one loss but a whole series of deprivations to which a person has to adjust. Growing old and retiring leads to a series of losses (physical, social and mental) especially in relation to the role and status of breadwinner, workmate, employee and relationship patterns within the family. Over a period of time other relationships are lost; family members may move away; people of one's own age group who live near you, or you played bowls or cribbage with, die; members of your family die. If you become housebound you lose contacts and become more dependent on family and friends to give you support, but you still will be able to adapt. In the case of children it is probably necessary to look at the quality of the relationship that is lost and not just the number of relationships.[1] So with the elderly, one may find that they can cope with the smaller number of relationships, provided they are sufficiently intense. The various forms of loss experienced by an elderly person after retirement may not all lead to a similar awareness of grief, but the accumulation of a large number of such 'minor' losses can lead to depression and reactions very similar to grief.

[1] Bowlby (1971) Ch. 2.

Grief is usually interpreted as both a reaction to loss and the *process* of realization by which we appropriate the loss ourselves and inwardly accept the reality of an event that has already occurred outside. It is a psychological process by which people fill the gap in their lives after a large part of their world has been lost. Grief has been defined as a 'deep or violent sorrow caused by loss or trouble'[1] and this reflects the idea that a part of our world is lost. Sorrow is seen as an essential ingredient of grief with an implied pining for the world which is lost, rather than the object itself. To describe it as a process rightly implies that we are thinking of something occurring over a period of time, and that its nature will change with time. Grief seems to run a more or less constant course but is modified mainly by the abruptness of the loss, the previous personality of the bereaved, the nature of the preparation for the loss, and the significance of the lost object to the person who is bereaved.

Much of the current literature deals with the grief reactions of people following the death of a loved one. Let us examine briefly these processes of normal grieving following a bereavement, and some of the problems that might arise. With this as a frame of reference we can look at some of the situations in a medical setting where people may experience loss, and see how far the insights gained from bereavement studies might help us to understand and support people experiencing other forms of loss.

Normal Grieving

After a Boston nightclub fire, E. Lindemann worked with the disaster victims and their families. As a result of this experience he was able to formulate several general classes of *normal grief*.[2]

Somatic distress. Somatic distress occurs in waves lasting from 20 minutes to one hour. There is deep sighing, lack of strength

---

[1] *Shorter Oxford English Dictionary.*   [2] Lindemann (1944) *101*, p. 141.

and appetite, choking sensations and breathlessness. Because the feelings are unpleasant and brought about by the person thinking and talking about the deceased, the bereaved person will therefore avoid such situations.

Preoccupation with the image of the deceased. Preoccupation with the image of the dead is very similar to day-dreaming. The bereaved may see and hear the deceased who is often found to be comforting. In one novel the reactions of a young widow are described:

The sky seemed full of him too, and he was part of the breaths she drew in, but he was also standing just behind her, looking over her shoulder. She wondered why she was not afraid, not of him, but of these things which she had never believed could happen. It was not the same as remembering Ben [her husband], or picturing him in her mind, it was a knowledge, that he was there. And most of all, he was there at moments when she had not been thinking of him: as she had come into this room, she had only been wondering which sheets to put on the bed for Jo, and whether it was at all damp. She said, 'Ben. I'm all right. Nothing else can happen. I can't be hurt. You're here, and Jo is here. It is all right'.[1]

Feelings of guilt. The bereaved will often say, 'If only...' and any ambivalent feelings concerning the deceased will often lead to exaggerated thoughts and actions. A parent of a child who was killed in a road accident said afterwards, 'If only I had made him wait while I brushed his hair he wouldn't have ended up beneath a car.'

Hostile reactions. Irritability, anger and loss of warmth towards others were other common reactions observed by Lindemann.

Losses in usual patterns of behaviour. The bereaved may move

[1] Hill (1974) p. 36.

about aimlessly and restlessly. Everything becomes an effort and there is a marked loss of zest. The activities that were shared with the deceased also lose their attractiveness, as do the relationships that were formed as a married couple rather than as a single person.

Adopting traits of the deceased. Traits of the deceased may appear in the behaviour of the bereaved. This phase may border on the pathological and sometimes the symptoms of the person who has died will be adopted by the bereaved together with any mannerisms shown by the deceased during the last illness.

Grief work

It was George Engel[1] who developed and built on the work of Lindemann and reintroduced the process of *grief work*. Grief work was described as the work of mourning by which we can become emancipated from bondage to the deceased, readjust to the environment in which the deceased is missing, and begin to form new relationships. This process consists of three phases: shock and disbelief, developing awareness and resolution. The whole process may take up to two years with a peak at the end of the first year. It is important that the bereaved should resolve their grief since unresolved grief can be the prelude to psychiatric illness.

Shock and disbelief. A phase of stunned numbness. 'Oh No! It isn't true'. A young woman whose husband died shortly after a major operation sat by his bed for some time talking to him, unable to accept that he was dead. Later she became angry with him for not responding to her and resisted efforts by staff to show her that he was dead. Slowly the realization dawned and she began to scold her husband for 'leaving her with two young

[1] Engel (1962).

children'. In this case the shock and disbelief lasted only a matter of hours, but it may last for several days. This phase is often described by the bereaved as a 'cotton wool' time when there seems to be an invisible blanket between you and the world around you. C. S. Lewis in his diary of personal grief writes about this phase:

At other times it feels like being mildly drunk, or concussed. There is a sort of invisible blanket between the world and me. I find it hard to take in what anyone says. Or perhaps, hard to want to take it in. It is so uninteresting. Yet I want the others to be about me.[1]

The form which the denial takes is influenced by cultural factors and by previous experience of loss and separation. One will find a whole range from verbal denial through to incapacitation.

Developing awareness. Pangs of grief come next, with intense periods of pining for the deceased, often accompanied by restlessness and aimless wandering and searching for the lost person.
    Crying and feelings of physical emptiness are also experienced in this phase together with acute sadness, apathy and exhaustion. C. S. Lewis described shaving as a great effort.

And no one ever told me about the laziness of grief. Except at my job—where the machine seems to run on much as usual—I loathe the slightest effort. Not only writing but even reading a letter is too much. Even shaving. What does it matter now whether my cheek is rough or smooth?[2]

Anger is also common and is frequently displaced in three

[1] C. S. Lewis (1961) p. 7.   [2] *Ibid.* p. 8.

main directions. Firstly it is directed against the deceased for deserting the family, secondly against others, for example the doctor, the ambulance service, the family or God and thirdly, personally, which may lead to attempts to inflict self-injury.

The anger against oneself is also linked to some extent with the strong guilt feelings that become evident in many cases with the feeling that somehow the bereaved must be responsible for the death or loss. Parents of handicapped children frequently pass through periods of blaming themselves and each other for the abnormality. It is at this stage that people often stop visiting and begin to lose interest. Staff may also feel the need to 'escape' and remember the urgent trip to the pharmacy or elsewhere. However, the bereaved need others around, not necessarily talking but willing to listen (to just BE there) and above all to accept and allow the expression of feeling, whether negative or not. While tranquillizing drugs may be necessary in some cases, there is a danger that being too ready to use sedation may lead to grief being postponed and not resolved.

Resolution. This stage completes the work of mourning and the establishment of a new identity, which may take many months. It is in this phase that many of the rites and rituals associated with mourning in society *may* help the recovery from the loss. We shall look at the way cultural factors may influence the grieving process in Chapters 7 and 8.

The process of resolution has several aspects. (1) The resolve that one *will* cope with the loss even though it is not easy to think of oneself as a 'widow'. (2) The frequent idealizing of the deceased. (3) The sense of detachment which comes from this idealization and which brings the ability to think and discuss the deceased realistically and comfortably. There can also be a new sense of freedom as voiced by the widow who bumped her car and said, 'Thank goodness I don't have to confess it to George'. (4) A final resolution when one can enjoy oneself again and make new social contacts, without feeling disloyal to the deceased. Here again cultural factors play a part in determining how soon a widow, for example, can 'decently' begin to go to social activities. To this end organizations such as *Cruse* and the *Society of Compassionate Friends*, can offer enormous support.

These three phases of shock and disbelief or denial, developing awareness and resolution are also reflected in the 'phases' described by other writers. The similarities between the descriptions of grief given by these different workers are shown in the table.

The phases of grief.

Phase	Engel[1]	Kubler-Ross[2]	Bowlby & Parkes[3]
1	Denial	Denial	Numbness
2	Developing awareness	Rage and anger Bargaining Depression	Pining Disorganization
3	Resolution	Acceptance	Re-organization

All the preceding references to 'phases' are really only a useful guide to the different stages that people may pass through. They are not meant to be clear-cut stages and it should be accepted that not everyone will pass through every phase in the same sequence, at the same pace, or with equal ease. However, they do provide us with a general framework with which to describe how people may reassess their world, and themselves in relation to it, following the experience of a major personal loss—and it must be stressed that unresolved grief can be the prelude to psychiatric illness.

[1] Engel (1962).   [2] Kubler-Ross (1970).   [3] Bowlby & Parkes (1970).

References and Further Reading

Bowlby, J. (1971) *Attachment and Loss*. Vol. 1, Attachment. Harmondsworth: Penguin.

Bowlby, J. & Parkes, C. M. (1970) Separation and Loss. In *The Child in His Family*, Vol. 1 of International Yearbook of Child Psychiatry and Allied Professions. ed. Anthony, E. J. & Koupernik, C. New York: John Wiley.

Engel, G. (1962) *Psychological Development in Health and Disease*. Philadelphia: W. B. Saunders.

Hill, S. (1974) *In the Springtime of the Year*. London: Hamish Hamilton.

Kubler-Ross, E. (1970) *On Death and Dying*. London: Tavistock Publications.

Lewis, C. S. (1961) *A Grief Observed*. London: Faber and Faber.

Lindemann, E. (1944) Symptomatology and management of acute grief. *Am. J. Psychiat.*, *101*, 141.

Shorter Oxford English Dictionary. (1970) London: Oxford University Press.

2 *Abnormal Reactions and Anticipatory Grieving*

For some people their grief may become exaggerated or distorted. There may seem to be little movement towards resolution of the grief and their reaction may then become pathological.

If the person can be prepared for the loss, in anticipation of it, then he or she may be enabled to meet the loss in a more constructive way.

Abnormal Reactions

Delay. Delay is the most common abnormal reaction and the postponement of grief may either be short or delayed for many years. This response often occurs if the death has happened at a time when the bereaved had to deny his or her own feelings in order to maintain the morale of others. People who have been involved in disasters may delay the expression of their grief because of the need to care for others. This delayed grief may find expression as an excessive reaction to a seemingly minor loss occurring many months or years later. For example, a young woman whose husband died following a car crash, in which she and her children were passengers, delayed her grief because of her concern to care for the children. Ten months later she dropped a favourite pottery ornament as a result of which she displayed a severe grief reaction.

Prolongation. Prolongation of grief is another problem, especially when the fact of the death has been denied. Loneliness and social isolation, with the attendant separation anxiety, often serve to heighten this problem.

Some of the distorted reactions that may be encountered are:

1. Excessive activity with no sense of loss.
2. Development of symptoms similar to those of the deceased, often with related psychosomatic illness.
3. Alteration in relationships with friends and relatives. All social contacts may be shunned and the person may become a recluse, or may need supervision because of giving away large sums of money.
3. Furious hostility against people associated with the death event, leading to letters of complaint and wishing to sue the hospital.
5. Behaviour resembling a schizophrenic pattern with lack of emotional expression, living in a daze, and acting in a 'wooden manner'.
6. Severe depression, with insomnia, guilt and bitter self-reproaches. Because the bereaved may feel the need to punish themselves for what has happened there is always an increased risk of suicide. 'I just want to die and be with him'.[1]

Other complicated forms of grief can arise as a result of the relationship where, for example, there may have been ambivalence or strong negative feelings may have been repressed. Lily Pincus is a psychotherapist and at 65 her life's work in the field of marital therapy was given a new direction when she herself was widowed.[2] She believes that marriages and relationships generally are based on two psychological principles: projection and identification.

People respond to bereavement in some measure according to which principle is stronger in their make-up. The couples who base their marital relationship on *projection* form complementary relationships in which the partners develop distinctly divided

---

[1] Lindemann (1944) *101*, p. 141.   [2] Pincus (1976).

roles. In the event of a bereavement such couples seem to cope with the loss of their partners, because they are more secure in their autonomy. The death of a spouse may become, after due mourning, a real time of growth and the survivor is often seen to 'take on a new lease of life'.

If, however, too much of the self was projected onto the now lost partner, and if the projection was rigidly maintained, then the bereaved cannot separate sufficiently from the lost partner to truly bury him and prolonged pathological mourning may result. The couples who built their marital relationship on *identification* and cannot bear to have differences find it especially hard to cope following bereavement. This would seem to be because they have little sense of personal worth to help them face the world without their marriage partner and they seem to become increasingly helpless.

Although atypical forms of grief do differ in intensity and duration from the more usual reactions to bereavement, certain aspects of which may be exaggerated or distorted, they do not differ in kind. There are no symptoms that are peculiar to pathological grief although it seems reasonable to view extreme expressions of guilt, identification symptoms (hypochondriacal illness), and delay in onset of grief of more than two weeks' duration, as indicators that the reaction to bereavement may take a pathological course.[1]

Anticipatory Grieving and Support

In 'crisis' theory[2] a technique of preventive intervention, called 'anticipatory guidance', is suggested as being helpful in adjusting to the impact of loss. The main aim of such guidance is to enable the person to cope by discussing the details of the impending crisis before it occurs. Such preventive intervention not only is of benefit to the individual awaiting the crisis, but it is

[1] Parkes (1975) p. 142.   [2] Caplan (1969) p. 56.

also helpful for those who will share the event whether as family or as members of the caring professions. The object of such guidance is to mobilize the person's strength beforehand so that it is possible to meet a loss more constructively. By being told in detail what to expect, and by imagining in advance what it might feel like, one is able to lower the anxiety level and develop a readiness for a healthy reaction. This concept has implications for staff-training programmes with the use of role-play and the expression of emotional reactions to various situations.

A good example of anticipatory guidance is that given in the form of antenatal classes where the mother-to-be (and father) are given information about the physical and emotional changes of pregnancy, labour and child development. Reassurance is given and many of the difficulties that can be encountered are discussed; for example mood changes, irritability and passivity, fears and superstitions, difficult labour and *sometimes* congenital abnormalities are mentioned. One can never fully prepare someone for an experience not yet theirs but some form of preparation can help the event to be a little less traumatic when it occurs, always provided that the picture formed is a realistic one and not too dogmatic![1]

The significance of this form of support in connection with loss is that it enables a realistic picture of the new world to be built up before the old one is destroyed. Therefore help

might be given where necessary to introduce the person undergoing the transition to the new opportunities open to him, and possibly to facilitate changes in his attitude by means of appropriate events ... to act as turning points in the process of realization.[2]

Where the family is undergoing anticipatory grieving care

[1] Kitzinger (1977) Ch. 3 and 15.   [2] Parkes (1975) p. 224.

may be needed to ensure that the patient does not become progressively excluded from the life of the family, 'Don't worry dear, we'll see to all that for you' or 'everything is being taken care of, just you forget it and leave it all to us'. This is not uncommon with the family of a patient with leukaemia where the various periods of remission have led to the family having finished much of their grieving before the patient dies. Resentment can then occur concerning the time spent coming to visit and caring for someone who should now be dead. This in turn leads to feelings of guilt and is not unrelated, in my opinion, to the pressure exerted by people for 'a quick end to it all'. Problems can arise if the anticipated loss does not occur.

The wife of a young patient diagnosed as being terminally ill underwent anticipatory grieving. The husband began to make a dramatic recovery as a result of which he had virtually to be reborn into the family unit once again.

In relation to patients facing surgical operations some very helpful work has been done, which examines the relationship between a person's worrying before operation to his or her behaviour after operation. If you talk to patients on a surgical ward before their operation it is possible to classify them into three groups.

Group I are those with a high degree of preoperative fear. These patients are constantly worried and suffer from insomnia. They often try to avoid or postpone the operation and only show a temporary response to reassurance from figures in authority.

Group II are those with moderate anticipatory fear. They are occasionally agitated and worried, and bothered about specific details of the operation, or the anaesthesia, but they can be given reassurance by someone in authority. For most of the time they are able to maintain an outward calm.

Group III is composed of a very optimistic group who are constantly cheerful. They will completely deny feeling and concern or worry, and do not seem to manifest any tension in their behaviour—they sleep well and are able to keep themselves well occupied in reading, socializing, and 'cheering up the others'.

In my own visits, as a chaplain, to surgical wards I have found it quite easy to identify these three groups of preoperative patients. In postoperative patients it has been found that those who are extremely fearful before the operation are more likely to be full of anxiety afterwards. The operation does not really affect their worries and in fact they worry about everything. Those who display a moderate amount of worry before going to the operating theatre are less likely to show any emotional disturbance afterwards. However, the group who have been most cheerful before the operation are the ones who give the doctors and nurses (and chaplain) most difficulty subsequently. They are much more likely to display reactions of anger and deep resentment as soon as they begin to experience the pains and other harassments that accompany the recovery from an operation.[1]

In a further study it was found that patients wanted to know what would happen to them and the sensations they might experience. It further emerged that being able to take an active part in their own recovery helped patients to feel less helpless. It was suggested that patients should be given precise and detailed information, although it was acknowledged that there could be difficulty in implementing the proposal.[2]

The principle that emerges from these studies is that before any crisis or loss occurs it helps if people can worry. But such worrying should be in relation to the reality of the situation. That is, one should stress the real detail of what will be perceived—if there will be pain after the operation, if the patient will smell anything (as for example with a stoma), or if they will feel sick, and what tubes they may have.

In an investigation into the relationship of preoperative preparation of patients to the postoperative stress and recovery, patients were given information about what was likely to

[1] Janis (1958) p. 130.   [2] Janis (1971) p. 102.

happen to them and the sensations that they might experience. They were also helped to talk about their feelings concerning hospitalization and they were taught exercises to perform after the operation. The study showed clearly that psychological preparation for an operation and the teaching of exercises to be performed after operation have a positive influence on the patients' postoperative condition.[1] The findings of this study show a clear parallel between anticipatory guidance for surgical patients and that already well established for antenatal patients.[2]

The nurse, doctor, social worker, chaplain or members of the patient's family can all play an important part in providing the anticipatory guidance that is both appropriate and acceptable, and which can help to reduce the amount of trauma that will accompany the event when it does occur. One does have to recognize, however, that there will always be a group of people who will worry excessively, however much preparation is offered to them!

References and Further Reading

Boore, J. R. P. (1977) Preoperative care of patients. *Nursing Times*, March 24, pp. 409–11.

Caplan, G. (1969) *An Approach to Community Mental Health*. London: Tavistock Publications.

Janis, I. L. (1958) Emotional inoculation: theory and research on effects of preparatory communications. In *Psychoanalysis and the Social Sciences*. New York: International Universities Press.

Janis, I. L. (1971) *Stress and Frustration*. New York: Harcourt Brace Jovanovich.

Kitzinger, S. (1977) *Education and Counselling for Childbirth*. London: Baillière Tindall.

[1] Boore (1977) pp. 409–11.   [2] Kitzinger (1977) Ch. 3.

Lindemann, E. (1944) Symptomatology and management of acute grief. *Am. J. Psychiat.*, *101*, 141.

Parkes, C. M. (1975) *Bereavement: Studies of Grief in Adult Life*. Harmondsworth: Penguin.

Pincus, L. (1976) *Death and the Family*. London: Faber and Faber.

3 The Courage to Remain Human

A young woman patient, who had suffered with leukaemia for several years, was readmitted to hospital. The ward staff knew her and her family very well, and were therefore upset when she eventually died on the ward. On the day when the patient died, the nurse in charge was a person who had formed a strong attachment to the patient and her husband since they were of a similar age group and had several interests in common. Immediately after the death, the nurse in charge attended to the patient and then went into the office, sat down, and wept. The patient's husband followed her into the office and said to her, 'You looked after her well and did all that could be done. Don't upset yourself so—I'll fetch you a cup of tea'.

The nurse told me later that she felt very guilty and a failure, both in her position on the ward and in not being supportive to the husband. The nursing structure, within which she worked, had taught her that 'experienced nurses' do not act in such a way and should not express their needs—especially whilst on duty. The husband, however, benefited greatly from this incident because it expressed to him the quality of the caring his wife had received and that staff had the courage to be human and to express their feelings. The husband was further helped by being able to get the nurse a cup of tea, and to offer help and support to one who had previously helped and supported so well both him and his wife.

Emotionally, open communication such as that just described is not something which comes easily. It is a two-way process in which the 'giver' has to learn to be a 'recipient', and the person who is usually designated as the provider of 'care' has to permit the recipient to contribute. Such caring can be costly in that it contains the possibility of being hurt and the need to recognize one's strengths and weaknesses. In the presence of the dying patient it also means facing the fact of one's own mortality, and one's own anxieties about death and dying.

The nursing structure has been said to be organized as a defence against increasing anxiety.[1] The way in which the work is done, and the way people act in a nursing unit, can reduce personal contact with patients and relatives.

In such a way the emotional stress and anxiety that can be generated by contact with suffering, disease and death can be lessened, but not altogether prevented. Many nurses have commented that the main place where they express any emotional reaction is in the privacy of their own bedrooms at the end of their 'shift'. But it is not only the nurses who may defend themselves against stress and anxiety, for other groups of staff may structure their work relationships similarly.

Loss and death, as already shown, are an ever present reality for medical and nursing staff whether they work in hospital or the community. A time of crisis for a patient or relative can also become a crisis for those who are caring for them. Those who choose to work in the caring professions usually have a desire to alleviate suffering and to help sick people become well again. If they fail to do so, this can generate a sense of failure and frustration which is especially evident when the patient is a child or a young adult.

It has been shown that patients who are facing death are formed of three broad groups who show different reactions.[2]

Those who have a firm religious faith, and practise regularly, are significantly less anxious about death and the dying process. Those who state that they have virtually no religious belief are similarly less anxious. Those who are unsure, lukewarm and hazy in their religious beliefs and who only attend a place of

[1] Menzies (1960) pp. 95–121.   [2] Hinton (1967) Ch. 7.

worship for a 'hatch, match and dispatch' ministry are the ones who exhibit most anxiety in relation to dying.

I believe that just as these three groupings are evident amongst the patients we care for, so they are evident amongst the staff. It is clear that for some people death is made more acceptable in the context of their own religious beliefs or philosophy of life. For example, within Christian teaching, death can paradoxically become part of the healing process. *I Corinthians* 15, v. 54: 'Death is swallowed up in victory' and *Revelations* 21, v. 4: 'he will wipe away every tear from their eyes, and death shall be no more, neither shall there be mourning nor crying, nor pain any more, for the former things have passed away'. This dimension of the subject of loss and grief implies the need for good communication between chaplain, staff and patient if the needs of all concerned are to be recognized and met.

Much of what has already been said about loss and grief, in relation to patients and their relatives, is also applicable in varying degrees to the staff who care for them. There are also various other factors within the staff/patient relationship which can lead to a shared experience of loss and grief.

Listening

One of the key words for staff who wish to help patients, and each other, to cope with their experience of loss and grief is *listening*. More importantly it is 'attentive listening' which implies being alert to the clues in the person's conversations that indicate a readiness to talk about the loss, or impending loss, of a limb/organ/function or of life itself. Sometimes it will be easier to *do* things to people rather than to *listen* to them and to share in their experience.[1] Much will depend on the sort of

---

[1] May (1969) p. 277. The conflicts are discussed which can arise for people who can take care *of* others without caring *for* them, can *direct* people but cannot *listen* to them.

relationship that has been built up, but listening to someone talk about their lost ideals and ambitions, as well as their achievements, is important.

A young woman, who was terminally ill, became very withdrawn. I visited her, as chaplain to the hospital, and gradually over many days built a relationship that enabled her to talk and to share. She told me that she felt she had 'only sipped at life and not drunk deeply'. She still had a year to go at University and had not yet qualified. She was engaged but not yet married. She said, 'I seem to be a potential person who has not yet achieved very much, and little time to do so.' From these conversations it was clear that she needed to gain a sense of personal worth and to feel that her life had some value. To this end it was important to include the family, the boyfriend, and the staff and to help them understand why she had withdrawn from contact with them.

Some people may not wish to talk to anyone about their reactions and clearly one cannot force people to talk! Likewise one should be wary of the temptation to tell people what you consider they should be thinking and feeling. Open-ended questions asking the person how he or she sees their situation at the present time will lead either to an expression of their feelings if they are prepared to talk or the reply, 'Fine, no problems' if they wish to close the subject. Patients will usually select the person they wish to talk to and it may well be a young and inexperienced staff member. Where there is good liaison between the various members of staff those less experienced should receive support from their colleagues if the patient relates to them. One hopes that senior staff will feel no resentment if the patient does not relate to them on the same level, but offer the necessary support to their colleagues. People's early contacts with death and loss can greatly influence their later attitudes, and it is important that they receive appropriate support at this early stage. This is especially true if the staff member has recently experienced a loss or a death in his or her own life.

Involvement

One reason for people finding it difficult to listen to what others are really saying is that it leads to one becoming involved. The more you know about someone and his family, the more he becomes a person. Such involvement is often actively discouraged on the grounds that it clouds judgement and in some situations this is clearly right. Close contact with someone who is trying to cope with loss and grief can lead to two opposite reactions:

Compassion. A response which leads one to move towards the patient with aid and comfort at varying levels.

Repulsion. A response triggered off by the threat of death and leading to a desire to retreat from the patient, to avoid contact, in order to protect oneself from the impending shock of the separation and loss.

The degree of success with which this conflict is resolved has implications for the quality of care that the patient ultimately receives. There are various ways in which staff may become involved with patients.

Identification. Most people have experienced loss or death in their own, or their family's, lifetime and so may find similarities which lead them to identify with the patient or a relative of the patient. A nurse who is caring for a young child with a congenital heart defect may find it is difficult to talk to the parents because he or she has a child with a similar problem who is to be operated on in the near future. The anxieties of the parents can quickly become an expression of his or her own. While this point of identity *could* be helpful it could also be a real barrier in that the nurse may want to sort out his or her reactions rather than those of the parents.

One aspect of identification, which is well known in the field of psychiatry, is that of transference and countertransference. By this is meant the transferring to one or more of the caring staff (usually at an unconscious level) the feelings and attitudes which originally belonged to important members of the patient's family group. The patient may thus transfer to the member of staff feelings of love or hate. The staff member may similarly identify in the patient attributes which belonged to important figures in the staff member's early life. If this is not recognized it can lead to over-involvement with loss of objective compassion or rejection.

Over-indulgence and over-protectiveness. If staff find themselves drawn to particular patients, especially children who are terminally ill, it is very easy to become over-protective. If the relatives are not thought to be very supportive then this can lead to animosity between staff and family. But the patient can also resent this. If the patient's mobility and independence has already been restricted by the illness or operation, such over-protectiveness by a staff member can be seen as a further restriction and thus can lead to anger.

Cross accusations. Tension may build up between staff because of the inability to cure or alleviate the suffering of a patient with whom they have become involved. This tension may lead to cross accusations of inefficiency and lack of care between members of staff, and they displace onto each other the anger or frustration they experience through looking after the patient.

Unresolved Grief

It can sometimes happen that staff move from one crisis to another, as can occur in special care units, and this can lead to the staff having much unresolved grief which can remain with them for many years. Sometimes there may be several deaths in quick succession and staff may be able to cope very well and without undue stress. On another occasion a close relationship may exist between patient and staff and the death becomes a personal failure and loss. If this happens several times, in a short period of time, the effect can be cumulative and the staff themselves may be visibly in need of support, and their morale declines. However, the opportunity for staff to work through, or even acknowledge, their feelings is rarely provided, and the need for this may be seen as a sign of weakness.

This is relevant not only within the hospital context, but also within the community. The length of time the patient is in hospital may be quite short, but the community staff may be required to give support for quite a long time—especially the general practitioner. A deep sense of loss may, therefore, be experienced on occasions following the death of a patient they have cared for over many months or years. If there is no opportunity to resolve their grief, the community staff may also carry their unresolved grief with them for many years.

Conclusion

It is too easy to take staff members for granted and to assume that they do not have needs. Because of this staff may suppress such needs and see them as inappropriate to their role. Some staff will be able to cope very well with personal loss and grief, and with that of their patients and colleagues. Such people can be a valuable asset provided their own ability to cope does not blind them to fact that others cannot. There would seem to be a need for some form of emotionally open support. Emotionally open communication with the patient often only appears when the mutual communication amongst the staff, or the relatives, is emotionally open too. This is not so surprising if we remember that the anxiety that often follows a more emotional contact with a patient can only be handled by nurses and doctors when they are able to talk about these emotions with each other.

This support, therefore, is offered by various people: the peer group, other professional colleagues, chaplain, friends and family—and on occasions the patient. In-service training needs to include ways of looking at the emotional climate of the ward, and the feasibility of extending such insights into everyday work. If such an activity cannot take place among the staff then it is not so likely to occur between the patient and the person caring for the patient. One is not suggesting a psycho-analytic session each day, or week, but that staff should ask one question of themselves, 'Why?' 'Why do I avoid Mr. X?' or 'Why can't I stop thinking about Margaret and her children when I go home?' As staff gain perspective of their own re-actions to loss they can explore, more confidently, ways of helping the patients and families they care for. In this way they may gradually learn to integrate death into the process of living, and thus find the courage and the confidence to remain human.

Summary of Concepts

Crises and losses are an important part of normal human development and contain within them the possibility of growth or regression. Crisis theory has implications for our experience of loss and grief in that the direction in which we move will depend largely upon the support we receive and the result of previous experience of loss and grief. This applies whether we are a patient or a member of staff caring for the patient.

Three stages of normal grieving may be identified: shock and disbelief; developing awareness; resolution. Some of the ab-normal reactions to grief have been discussed. The concept of 'anticipatory support' is seen as one way of mobilizing the patient's or staff member's strengths beforehand so that when the loss is experienced he or she may be better able to cope with it constructively.

References and Further Reading

Hinton, J. (1967) *Dying*. Harmondsworth: Penguin.

May, R. (1969) *Love and Will*. London: Souvenir Press.

Menzies, I. (1960) A case study in the functioning of social systems as a defence against anxiety. *Hum. Relat.*, *13*, 95–121.

Part Two
Loss and Grief in Medicine

4 *Obstetrics and Gynaecology*

Obstetrics

Most expectant parents know the hopes, the plans and the dreams that they have for their baby. The mother also knows of the backache, the discomfort from the baby's elbow under the ribs, and the occasional fears that all may not go well. However well-adjusted a couple may be there are times when apprehensive thoughts may enter their minds—perhaps following a television programme, or an article in a magazine, or a poster in the antenatal clinic warning that 'Smoking harms your baby'. Usually the mother can shake off these anxieties and will refuse to believe that such things could ever happen to *her* baby. For the majority all goes well and the baby is born with the right number of fingers and toes, with dad's hair colour or eyes, and other family characteristics. Everyone displays pleasure, and the father rushes off to telephone the good news. The earlier fears are now only a vague memory and soon forgotten as the parents look upon a perfect infant asleep in the cot.

When a woman is in travail she has sorrow, because her hour has come; but when she is delivered of the child, she no longer remembers the anguish, for joy that a child is born into the world.[1]

[1] *St John's Gospel* 16, *v.* 21.

But, sometimes, the earlier fears of pregnancy become a reality and all is not well at birth. It may be a heart murmur that is expected to correct itself later, or a minor deformity that can be corrected by later surgery, or a predicted Rhesus baby which can be transfused. It may be a major abnormality, either detected during pregnancy or quite unexpected. Sometimes the child may be stillborn.

Whatever the defect, and however easily it may be corrected, there will be for the parents a great sense of loss and failure which will lead to expression of grief. The staff who are looking after the parents also share in the sense of loss. The way in which we cope with the grief will depend largely upon our own personalities, on the support received, and the way in which we have coped with previous experiences of loss and grief.

Spontaneous abortion and stillbirth

There are many similarities between the reactions to a stillbirth and the reactions to a spontaneous abortion. If the pregnancy is a planned one, and the couple have been looking forward to the birth of the baby, then the distinction between stillbirth[1] and spontaneous abortion[2] is an academic one. What is important *to them* is the loss of the child they were expecting. Even if the pregnancy was not planned we cannot assume that the child was not wanted or that there will not be a sense of loss for the parent, especially if the event occurs during the later stages of pregnancy.

Spontaneous abortion or miscarriage. It is difficult to know how many women experience spontaneous abortion because the baby may be lost before they realize they are pregnant. They

[1] A child born dead after the twenty-eighth week of pregnancy. In 1975 there were 10.3/1000 total births.
[2] Commonly referred to as a 'miscarriage' and occurring in the first 28 weeks of pregnancy.

may therefore think that they have had a late and possibly heavy period.

Most women probably do not need or want counselling, and manage to cope with the experience of miscarriage. At the same time, there are frequently dark moments—often in the middle of the night—and it is then particularly that a woman tends to look for causes of the miscarriage and to explain it by remembering that she slipped and fell on the stairs or that she had intercourse the night before.... On the whole contemporary medical opinion is that although environmental stress can affect uterine function through secretion of hormones, such incidents rarely cause miscarriage. The counsellor may explain that the cause is more likely to be that there was abnormal development of the fetus, or in the remaining cases, where the fetus was normal, that the woman ran a very high temperature with an infection, or that there was something inhospitable about the lining of the uterus in which, the counsellor can say, the fetus embeds itself rather like a plant with its roots in the soil.[1]

Although statistically one may be able to tell the parents that a future pregnancy should be all right, this information should not be used as a means of avoiding the expression of any distress that the mother and father may be feeling. 'Don't upset yourself, dear. You're young and you can have lots of babies.' In the early weeks of a pregnancy the mother may not really be aware that she is pregnant, but after about three months the awareness increases and so proportionately does the sense of loss and resultant grief. If the pregnancy was not planned and the mother expresses relief that it is ended it is not unusual for her also to feel some guilt for not wanting it, and to wonder if she may in some way have caused the miscarriage.

The father of the child can often find it irritating and disquieting to see his wife upset and may feel at a loss to know

[1] Kitzinger (1977) pp. 272–3.

what to do. After a few days he may start to avoid her, and any talk of the miscarriage, by working late or 'going off with his mates'. He may tell her to 'pull herself together' and take her off on holiday as his effort to put things right. Sometimes it will work very well, but it may instead make the woman feel that she is being 'bought off' that her feelings are not being valued, although she may realize that he is acting with the best of intentions. The loss experience is not being shared and this can lead to a cycle of recrimination, resentment, misunderstanding and marital stress.

The man may also blame himself and feel that his virility and masculinity have been threatened by his inability to produce a live child. The pressure from family and friends, to prove themselves reproductively capable, can be an added strain at this time. Intercourse can then cease to be 'love making' and instead become a planned mechanical exercise.

Some women become anxious and protective about their bodies, keenly aware of all physical sensations, and so disappointed as each menstrual period comes that they feel the inconvenience and the discomfort of the contracting uterus much more intensely than before. Each period then becomes for them a sort of miscarriage, and with the first signs of bleeding they mourn again yet another lost baby. Some react hysterically; that is, they have physical illnesses which are psychosomatic in origin. One of these hysterical illnesses is *pseudocyesis*, or phantom pregnancy. The woman misses her period, sometimes for months on end, swells up, and often has nausea and vomiting and other signs of pregnancy, but is not pregnant at all. She is not pretending; she honestly believes she is pregnant. In other cases there may be a severe emotional imbalance, linked with the painful feelings of loss, which lead a woman to take another woman's baby. What she is suffering then corresponds to puerperal depression, but in this case depression is on the actual experience of loss.[1]

---

[1] *Ibid.* p. 275.

A miscarriage can often make a woman feel that she is a *failure as a woman*, and thus she needs to regain a sense of worth and confidence in herself. The husband has a very important part to play in this and loving, tender care is often the best medicine. Those who are caring for the family may find it necessary to help the husband respond appropriately and to *share* the experience with his wife. The woman may also require guidance in allowing her husband to share her grief and to express his. In most stable relationships this works itself out without any intervention being necessary, but knowing that help and support is available can in itself be of great benefit.

Stillbirth. Stillbirth is a tragedy for the parents and for those who are looking after them at the time. When the death occurs before delivery there is always the dilemma of what to tell the parents and at what stage. If the fetal death has been diagnosed some time before the mother can be delivered of the child the distress is increased. Even if the mother is not told a great deal, she frequently comments later that she knew because of the expressions on people's faces as they sought to find the fetal heart beat, and by the lack of movement of the baby inside her.

Within the labour ward there is usually a quietness and a sadness as the child is delivered, hurriedly wrapped in a sheet and taken away. There is no joy, only a strong sense of failure. The unexpected stillbirth leads to a similar scene, except for the moments of frantic resuscitation during which time the anxieties of all present increase. The delivery of a dead child is the antithesis of all that the labour ward stands for and it engenders a feeling of incompetence in those involved which can easily lead to poor communication and withdrawal from the scene. Sometimes the chaplain will be informed and asked to help the parents work through their grief, but often a referral is not made if the chaplain is seen as 'a symbol of medical failure'. Quite often the parents are left to their own devices because this episode of loss represents a threat to those associated with it who may wish to deny or postpone any feelings of grief that they may have.

Distress can almost be like a contagious disease[1] in that it raises feelings of anxiety in those involved with people in distress.

Anxiety is catching, and its expression is repellent rather than attractive. Unless there is a prior bond of love or commitment to an anxious person, most of us will try to avoid him, or seek a quick escape from the infection of anxiety. If we do not literally cross the road to avoid him, we find ourselves remembering an urgent appointment, or we buy the sufferer a drink and perhaps have one ourselves. In the consulting room, the doctor or psychiatrist finds himself prescribing a sedative instead of making time to listen to the patient's story.[2]

However, those who have a professional commitment to the family of a stillborn child have to overcome these feelings if they are to offer support and enable the family to use the experience constructively. Failure to do so can lead to unresolved grief and problems in a subsequent pregnancy. Heavy sedation, unless absolutely necessary, usually only postpones the grief and may make it harder to accept the reality of what has happened. Parents in this situation seem to pass through the same grief process as that outlined in Chapter 1.

Shock and disbelief: developing awareness: resolution. When the mother is first told she often exclaims, 'Oh no! It isn't true, tell me it isn't true!' One mother who knew that her child had died before her induced labour said, 'I had an empty feeling within my tummy. I was numb and couldn't believe that the life within me had ceased to be. My baby just went stiff'.

Gradually the mother and father became aware of what has happened and there is a period of intense pining for the child. 'I want my baby, what have you done with him?' This is often accompanied by aimless wandering around, if physically able to

[1] Speck (1976) p. 42.   [2] Mathers (1970) p. 20.

do so. Being near to other mothers and babies can help some bereaved mothers, but can be agonizing to others. Some women say later that they would rather see another baby in the post-natal ward where they feel safe, rather than in the supermarket where she may want to take it home, and find that others do not understand.

Crying is important and a distinction should be made between *allowing* someone to cry and *saying they should* cry, which can make them feel guilty if they cannot. Feelings of physical emptiness and apathy are also common and can distress the husband. For example, his wife may need a lot of encouragement to tidy her hair or clean her teeth.

At various times during the grief process the parents may express anger. 'Why me? Why has God taken *my* baby, it has done no wrong. It's not fair when many get rid of their baby'.

Anger is usually displaced in three directions, and has the overall effect of repulsing people. It may be directed against the deceased for having died. 'You know we wanted you, why did you have to die,' or against others; 'Why couldn't the doctor/midwife get him to breathe', 'Why did God allow it', or the husband may blame his wife and say, 'It's all your fault, you should have stopped smoking'. The parents may direct the anger against themselves. This can sometimes lead to self-harm because they feel responsible for the death. A young father whose wife had given birth to two abnormal stillborn children subsequently committed suicide, and in a note left by him he explained that he felt genetically responsible for their death and that his wife would be better without him.

How can we cope with such anger? An instinctive reaction is to try to soothe and pacify the person, or to become defensive about the care received or about ourselves, or to retreat. However, there is a need to help the person to express their anger and see it as a normal response. To this end it can help if we ask ourselves, 'Why is this person angry and how can I help them to withstand it?'

One source of hurt and anger for patients is when they are

told 'Well, you are young, you can always have more children' or 'Well, at least you didn't get to know him or her'. However well meaning people are in making such remarks they still hurt and are sometimes interpreted as an insult to the child who has died. The mother and father have known the baby as a fact in their minds for the period of gestation. Even if the baby is born dead, he or she has already existed and is a person to be grieved for, although there is no *body* for the parents to touch and to hold to help them fix their baby in reality. It is at this point that we have to be sensitive in our care for the parents. They should not be encouraged to deny the existence of the baby and their relationship to it, for this can lead to difficulties in subsequent pregnancies.[1]

Not all parents will want to see the baby but it can often help if they do. Dr Hugh Jolly describes a young houseman, after only two months at the Charing Cross Hospital, being able to help a mother who was afraid to look at her stillborn child and to accept the reality of its existence.

He sat on her bed and talked to her. The baby was there, wrapped in a green cloth. After a while, she was able to feel first the baby's foot through the cloth, and gradually the whole body; then the baby was uncovered.

The mother should be told if she is to be delivered of a fetus that has died in utero, said Dr Jolly. The obstetrician, the midwife, the nurses know what has happened; Dr Jolly believes that the mother, too, often does know, for women have described to him how they felt when the baby had 'gone stiff'. Yet the pretence is kept up; under such circumstances, the atmosphere in the delivery room is wrong. As one woman put it: 'I was giving death, not birth, and I wanted to know'.[2]

The final phase of the grieving process does come eventually,

[1] E. Lewis (1976) p. 620.   [2] Jolly (1976) p. 4.

although there may well be periods when the couple feel depressed or angry. But, gradually they become involved with work and their family once again. The funeral can often help to facilitate the grief process, especially if the father and mother have talked together about the funeral arrangements. So often it is expedited while the mother is in hospital to save her upset. The father collects the certificate of stillbirth (or death certificate if the baby was born live and died soon after), and goes to register the birth and death and to arrange the funeral. It is not unusual to find that it is all completed without the mother knowing anything about it. It can help if the certificates can be retained for 48 hours, to allow the mother to recover from the delivery and for husband and wife to be encouraged to discuss the arrangements together. Should we always assume that the husband is the strong partner who can cope with all this on his own? We must also ask ourselves what support *he* needs. The D.H.S.S. circular allowing hospitals to make all the arrangements may help some families, but it can also facilitate the family's detachment from what has happened.[1]

The following letter to a nursing journal shows the positive outcome of courageously sharing and facing together the reality of a stillborn child.

This year I had a Caesarean section at term, when I had a baby boy who lived only six hours. For two or three weeks before I had a feeling or instinct that something was wrong, which I would not even admit to myself. When I came round from the anaesthetic, I knew without being told that the baby had died.

Naturally, I was heartbroken, until I learned from the results of the postmortem examination that he had had a severe atrial-septum defect with gross respiratory distress. Having done some student nurse training, including three months obstetrics, I knew how poor his prognosis would have been for living a normal healthy life, but this was never put to me by the staff.

[1] DS 211/75 which comments on HM(72)4.

Although I never saw the baby, my husband had a glimpse of him and was able to tell me that he had long, dark hair and the staff said he was a big bonny baby weighing over 4 kg. Having worked with many normal babies, I was able to build up a picture of him that is sufficient for my needs.

He was christened so, when the question of the funeral arose, my first thought was that it would have to be delayed until I was out of hospital. My family agreed. When I told the staff that I was going to the funeral the reaction, especially among the older members of staff, was surprise, and they questioned my decision, causing me to have second thoughts. But I stuck to my decision.

My own, young G.P. agreed with me, although he said it would take courage.

My husband had accidentally seen, on a visit to the undertakers, the dimensions and description of the tiny coffin, so I was able to visualize it, which was a great help because it was the size which shocked my family most.

I felt relief after the service. A chapter in our lives had been closed. I had carried him for nine months, looked forward to his birth, knitted for him, our lives revolving around my pregnancy. All we could do for him was a service and a nice headstone to mark his grave, which bears only his name and a quotation. No dates. My husband and I, indeed our families, feel that the chapter was closed carefully on a completed story and we can now look forward with healthy anticipation to our next child.

(Name and address supplied)[1]

Much of what has been written in this section on stillbirth and spontaneous abortion can also be applied to many of the people who have their pregnancies terminated. While many do not show a very marked grief reaction at the time, I have found that a subsequent admission to hospital for a seemingly minor procedure often triggers-off a feeling of remorse. This is seen at its strongest in those women who have had a termination earlier

[1] *Nursing Mirror* (1976).

in life and who later experience difficulty during a future pregnancy, or in trying to conceive.

Infertility

Infertility is another area where one meets couples who may show a fairly marked grief reaction to the fact that they are unable to conceive. This can still occur, to some extent, even when the sterilization has been sought by one or other of them. This is one reason for careful selection of people for vasectomy or tubal ligation, with appropriate counselling. A couple who cannot conceive, for whatever reason, may well feel a loss of function, or a loss of status and purpose, and in some relationships they may feel a loss of desirability which can lead to impotence. However, as I hope to show in relation to grief following the birth of an abnormal child, the grief process is often delayed because of the strong element of *hope* that perhaps there will be a new drug or technique to help them conceive and bear a child.

Congenital abnormality

When a baby is born with a defect[1] there usually follows a grief process very similar to that already described, because the parents are grieving for the normal child that they have *lost*. But the grief process is very much affected by the fact that before you can satisfactorily work through your grief you have to care for the child (the abnormal child) who is the cause of your grief. It is not surprising, therefore, that parents frequently find it hard to accept the abnormal baby as their own.

Initially the parents, shocked and disbelieving, may refuse to accept that there is anything wrong with their baby. 'You've

[1] In 1975 there were 18.9/1000 total births (live and stillborn).

brought me the wrong baby' or 'I don't want him any more, I thought he was all right until you told me he was a mongol'. This leads to guilt and anger, with the placing of blame as previously mentioned: 'If only I had been more careful during pregnancy, and stopped smoking'. Similarly a mother who was admitted to an antenatal ward or a gynaecological ward for 'bed rest' as a threatened abortion may wonder if it wouldn't have been better to have stayed at home and taken the risk. However, at the time of admission she probably felt otherwise. One mother said to me, 'I eat a lot of chips and I wonder if that gave my baby spina bifida because that's what the papers say—it's caused by potatoes'.

The shock and denial may last for months or years, and is often a way of handling feelings of failure and shame. One mother did not take her baby out in the pram for nearly a year because she felt people's reactions and comments would make her realize it was abnormal. Weeping and feelings of loneliness may persist for longer than if the child had died. 'I felt, and still feel, that I'm the only woman to have an abnormal baby. I'm a failed mother, a leper. People tend to avoid me in the shops if the baby is with me because they don't know what to say when they look in the pram, so I keep to myself'.

As the parents become more aware of the baby's condition there is a danger that they can become over-protective and over-indulgent. One father expressed his own unhappiness that since the birth of their child (who had a heart lesion) his marriage was under strain. He explained that his wife spent a great deal of time cuddling the baby and at bedtime took the baby to bed and placed the baby between the husband and wife. He felt guilty that he was growing more resentful of the child and found it hard to explain his feelings to his wife.[1]

Hope is more prevalent in parents with an abnormal child since they hope for a miraculous cure of the defect. Sometimes this leads to 'shopping around' different hospitals and doctors

[1] See also Tew et al. (1977).

hoping for a different diagnosis. They may also ask advice on spiritual healing, and the possibility of going to Lourdes or other healing centres. While many parents receive great help and support in this way, it does for many lead to a delay in the grief process, unless they are enabled to accept the reality of the situation. The healing centres can sometimes be instrumental in helping people to come to terms with reality and enabling the parents to cope. The birth of a child with congenital abnormalities would seem to lead to an 'open-ended' grief, because the handicapped child reminds the parents of the normal child they do not have. Many parents are able to live with this fact and to give a great deal of love and care to their child. However, they do themselves also require a great deal of understanding and support.

Coping with feelings. What can staff do to help the parents, and how can staff cope with some of their own feelings?

In one word—*listen*! Allow the parents to express any ambivalent feelings about the baby or any feelings of failure. It can help to say, 'You may have many mixed feelings about your baby'. We must try not to be shocked by some of the things the parents may say. For example, a father may ask the doctor to 'put the child out of its misery' and may offer a donation to research if he agrees. As a chaplain I find that I sometimes have to help parents to talk to each other because of the feelings of hurt that have made them withdraw into themselves. Telling the parents what you know about the child's condition is important and not doing so is a great source of subsequent complaint. One parent explained that they had been under the impression that their child 'had brain damage' for several years and that they felt a great deal of frustration at not being told anything. Further, they said that what they had been told was in such big words that they couldn't understand it.[1] Great

---

[1] Hannam (1975) Ch. 2, where several examples are given by parents of mentally handicapped children.

sensitivity is needed, and often staff are not sure of the actual diagnosis and therefore may justifiably be reluctant to say too much. However, if there is a strong indication that the child has an abnormality, it is frequently better to share this with the parents and to gradually reveal more information, as it is available and when it is thought that the parents are ready for it.

The grief process is often helped by encouraging the mother or father and baby contact from the beginning. In some units it is the practice to show the mother the baby and to discuss the baby's condition. Again great sensitivity is required in this as with the stillborn child. It is not easy to establish a link with your baby through a pane of glass and an incubator, and encouraging the mother to feed and care for her baby in the premature baby unit (as many already do) can be beneficial. The child's father also needs help and support, and may require encouragement to share in the care of the child at this early stage.

Our feelings, as staff, in such situations are affected by our own experience of loss and we should not deny our reactions. This is especially true when there has been a maternal death. When such an event occurs there is need for staff to have the opportunity to express *their* feelings if they are to be able to offer support to the patient's family. It is not so much a matter of being uninvolved as *controlling* the degree of our involvement. The most common defence is to withdraw or to say as little as possible. It is only as we feel able to *be with* someone as opposed to going *to do things* to that person.

One can summarize the ways in which staff can assist the mourning process as:

Supporting the patient's existing coping mechanisms.

Helping the patient to express feelings when ready to do so.

Helping the patient to continue as normal a life as possible. This means preventing other forms of loss. If the patient can go to the toilet, and there is no reason for not doing so, then not giving the patient a bedpan and thus reducing independence.

Providing privacy as necessary.
Maintaining resources of support by including the family as far as possible.
Prevent feelings of abandonment.
Recognize when the mourning reaction is becoming abnormal and obtaining appropriate additional help.
Create an emotionally open atmosphere for staff to express their feelings, as well as the patient.[1]

The tensions that are often present in such situations will often reach a peak when it is decided to withdraw the active treatment of a particular infant. This is always a painful decision for staff to make, and many of the tensions seem to arise from the *way in which* the decision is made. Many problems can be avoided if a team approach is adopted, and the nurses, doctors and others concerned are given an opportunity to ventilate their feelings and to be included in the decision-making process. It is also helpful if seminars can be arranged on an interdisciplinary basis to discuss some of the issues involved. An emotionally open communication between staff can help to create the right atmosphere for a more emotionally open communication with the parents.[2]

Gynaecology

In the field of gynaecology the two most common events which can lead to feelings of loss are the menopause and the hysterectomy operation.

Menopause

The menopause is an event that each woman must experience as a normal part of her growth and development. Apart from

[1] This list is adapted from that suggested by Carlson (1970) p. 112.
[2] *Ibid.* Ch. 3.

the physical symptoms that may be experienced, the changes in the reproductive organs can sometimes have a marked effect on the marital relationship. Although the capacity to enjoy sexual relationships continues in both sexes after fertility has ceased, some women may still feel that they will not be as attractive once they cannot bear children. If there has been any marital disharmony the couple may treat the menopause as the end of a sexual life which had never been fully realized or enjoyed. For others, the menopause can lead to a renewal of affection and a new freedom in their relationship. This is often linked to feelings that one stage of life is ended but that a new status with new opportunities is developing. Hence it does not always follow that the menopause will be accompanied by equally strong feelings of loss and grief in all women, whether they are married or single.

Hysterectomy

An equally varied response is to be found in women who undergo a hysterectomy operation. Much depends on the age of the woman, her mental and physical health, and her relationship if she is married. Several articles have been written in recent years in an attempt to establish whether one can define a pre-hysterectomy syndrome or a posthysterectomy syndrome.

A study of 200 women who had had a hysterectomy showed that 55% of the women operated on under the age of 40 years had postoperative depression.[1] In a further study, comparing women who had a hysterectomy performed with those undergoing other surgical operations, such as cholecystectomy, appendicectomy and mastectomy, postoperative depression was more commonly found in the hysterectomy group.[2] There were also indications that the operations performed for slight indications were more likely to lead to severe depression

---

[1] Richards (1973) p. 430.   [2] Richards (1974) p. 983.

subsequently. This was more marked in the depression or anxious patient who had tried to pressure her doctor for the operation as the 'only answer' to her gynaecological problems.

It has been suggested that we should recognize a 'pre-' rather than a 'post-' hysterectomy syndrome so that women at risk of severe postoperative depression can be recognized and cared for before their operation.[1]

The use of a term such as 'prehysterectomy syndrome' implies that there is a group of symptoms and causes not easy to isolate. It is, therefore, not easy to isolate all the forms of loss (anticipated and realized) that a woman may experience at this time.

The most commonly experienced loss is that resulting from the knowledge that she can no longer conceive and bear children, and that her reproductive life is over. The possibility of a pregnancy may have added meaning, and an element of risk, to intercourse for some couples. When the possibility of conception is removed there may be a very real sense of loss, which in some instances can lead to impotence. The earthy jokes that may abound on some gynaecological wards are often a cover for the fears of loss of sexual urge (libido) which patients may find difficult to discuss. Associated with the loss of libido can be insomnia and lethargy. If there has been tension in the marital relationship the operation, as with menopause, can then become the focus for marital disharmony and the ending of sexual relationships. In my experience as a chaplain I have been asked by women to talk to their husbands and to explain that they can no longer expect to have intercourse with their wife because of the operation. Subsequent discussion with medical and nursing staff has shown that they too have had similar requests from the same patient to conspire in misleading the husband, and the need for appropriate counselling has been apparent.

Such experiences of loss do not always lead to severe grief reactions for there are many women, who have a known

[1] Hunter (1974) p. 1266; Ballinger (1977) p. 83.

malignancy, or severe endometriosis, who are glad to have the operation. They frequently say that they will be glad when it is all over and they 'will feel better'. Additionally there are many who look forward to a new lease of life in which they can enjoy their marital relationship without any fear of pregnancy.

In the Middlesex Hospital in London a pamphlet has been devised for patients who attend the gynaecology clinic and who are to undergo a hysterectomy operation for non-malignant causes. The aim of the pamphlet is to enhance the verbal communication between staff and patient, and to improve the level of anticipatory guidance and understanding. The information on the leaflet includes:

Why necessary to admit as soon as possible.
Full explanation of the operation.
No menstruation or pregnancy after the operation.
Change of life—depending on removal of ovaries, etc.
Operation will not affect the appearance cosmetically or personal relationship with husband.
Their scar—cosmetic effect.
Wound drains.
Postoperative discomfort and length of time in hospital.
Convalescence and return to normal life.

Such forms of anticipatory guidance, in addition to the recognition of a prehysterectomy syndrome, can be very helpful in enabling people to readjust to some of the losses they may experience before and after a hysterectomy operation.

Summary

The stages of grief, identified by Engel, provide a way of understanding the experience of loss following a stillbirth and suggest ways of helping the parents accept the reality of the child's existence. When a baby is born with congenital abnormalities there is a similar reaction of shock and disbelief followed by a growing awareness. However, their grief is usually 'open-ended'. The need to listen and to share as openly as possible what is known about the child has also been stressed. Certain groups of women seem to be predisposed to depression and a deep sense of loss following a hysterectomy. Anticipatory support and preoperative screening to identify those people at most risk may help them to face and cope with the experience better.

References and Further Reading

Ballinger, C. B. (1977) Psychiatric morbidity and the meno-pause: survey of a gynaecological out-patient clinic. *Br. J. Psychiat.*, *131*, 83–9.

Carlson, C. E. (1970) *Behaviour Concepts and Nursing Intervention.* Philadelphia, U.S.A.: Lippincott.

Department of Health and Social Security (1975) *Funerals for Stillborn Infants.* DS 211/75. London: H.M.S.O.

Gath, A. (1977) The impact of an abnormal child upon parents. *Br. J. Psychiat.*, *130*, 405–10.

Hannam, C. (1975) *Parents and Mentally Handicapped Children.* Harmondsworth: Penguin.

Hunter, D. J. S. (1974) Effects of hysterectomy. *Lancet, ii,* 1266.

Jolly, H. (1976) Stillbirth—a new approach. *Nursing Mirror,* October 7, p. 4.

Kitzinger, S. (1977) *Education and Counselling for Childbirth.* London: Baillière Tindall.

Lewis, E. (1976) The management of stillbirth—coping with unreality. *Lancet, ii,* 620.

Mathers, J. (1970) The context of anxiety. In *Religion and Medicine I.* ed. Melinsky, H. London: S.C.M. Press.

Letter—on stillbirth. (1976) *Nursing Mirror,* October 21, p. 44.

Richards, D. H. (1973) Depression after hysterectomy. *Lancet*, *ii*, 430.

Richards, D. H. (1974) A posthysterectomy syndrome. *Lancet*, *ii*, 983.

Speck, P. W. (1976) The relative nuisance. In *Religion and Medicine III*. ed. Millard, D. London: S.C.M. Press.

Tew, B. J., Laurence, K. M., Payne, H. & Rawnsley, K. (1977) Marital stability following the birth of a child with spina bifida. *Br. J. Psychiat.*, *131*, 79–82.

5 *General Surgery*

The prospect of surgery is not something that is welcomed by many people, although the necessity of it may be readily acknowledged when pain and discomfort have been experienced for some time.

If the patient has had pain for a long while before admission to hospital he or she may say that they will be glad to be rid of the offending or diseased part of the body. An example of this is the patient who has experienced difficulty with the blood supply to the lower limbs. The leg later becomes gangrenous and has to be removed. If the patient has had a great deal of pain it is not unusual for him or her to *ask* the surgeon to remove it. Because most would agree that it is right to remove the limb it is tempting to assume that there will be little psychological reaction to the amputation 'because the patient has requested it'. Some recent studies, however, have indicated that, in the case of limb loss, one can sometimes identify a reaction that is comparable to that which we normally designate as 'grief'.[1] A parallel reaction is that of the potential widower who hopes that his wife will soon die and be 'released' from the agony she is suffering. When she does die he will still grieve for the loss, and may also feel guilty because of the relief he feels that the burden of watching her suffer is lifted.

[1] Parkes (1975) p. 204.

Closely related to the topic of surgical loss is the concept of *body image*, by which is meant the picture of our own body as it appears to ourselves in our own mind.[1] This is a simplified definition of the term which may conveniently describe how we experience and perceive our own bodies and organs and limbs, and how the experience of loss may change this body image. The young child, as he or she develops, will gradually build up attitudes and social perceptions of his body through interaction with other people. The parental attitudes will be especially important in forming a concept of 'myself', 'my body' and how it works. Depending upon the child's experience, various parts of the body will be seen as good or bad, clean or dirty, liked or disliked, mentionable or unmentionable. Such attitudes are an integral part of the body image. If the body image is disrupted by amputation, or other surgery, it can lead to a grief-like reaction which requires a period of mourning before the resulting trauma is resolved and a new, acceptable, body image is formed. The acceptance of this by others is an important part.

With the exception of limb loss, there has not been a great deal written concerning the patient's reactions to other forms of surgical loss. However, it is becoming clearer that the psychological preparation of patients for operation can have a positive influence on their postoperative condition.[2] In this chapter we shall look at a selection of surgical procedures where a loss is experienced together with ways in which guidance and support may be of benefit to patient, family and staff.

Mastectomy

Ann was 30 years of age and unmarried when she read a magazine article about breast cancer. The article included details of how to

---

[1] Schilder (1935).
[2] See p. 17 and the discussion on anticipatory guidance. A useful survey of some of the research relating to the preoperative care of patients is contained in Boore (1977).

examine the breast for lumps. She decided that perhaps she should examine herself, although she had never given much thought to it before. When she did so she was alarmed to find what seemed to be a lump. At first she tried to convince herself that it wasn't there, that she had made a mistake. Perhaps it would go away. She did not go to the doctor immediately in case he confirmed her worst fears. Over the next few days she tried not to think about it and threw the magazine away. She forgot all that had been said about cysts and found that she was becoming more sure that she had cancer, and so she decided she would not have peace of mind until she saw her doctor.

Ann's doctor examined her and agreed that she did have a lump and that he would arrange for her to attend at the local hospital where a biopsy could be performed, and the nature of the lump ascertained. He reassured Ann that the lump need not be a malignancy and—as she had expressed the fear—that it might not lead to her losing a breast. At the hospital she signed a consent form for a biopsy and 'any other necessary procedure arising from the biopsy'. At this stage she admitted that, although it was explained that they may wish to proceed to a mastectomy, her mind would only focus on the biopsy and seem to close to other possibilities.

When Ann awoke from the anaesthetic she was alarmed to find a large dressing instead of the small plaster she expected. She also noticed that she was 'flat on one side' and she felt 'that they had taken advantage of me, while I was asleep, to ruin me'. The house officer was on the ward at the time and, at the staff nurse's request came to talk to Ann. He explained that they had done the biopsy as promised, but that the initial examination in theatre had indicated the need to proceed with the mastectomy. He also reassured her that they felt confident in having removed all of the tumour and that, whilst they would wish her to have some radiotherapy treatment, he was sure that she would make an excellent recovery.

Her mind was in a whirl and many thoughts came to her. 'They have mutilated me and I shall look hideous'. 'Why should this happen to me at my age, it's not fair?' 'How can I expect any boyfriend to want to go out with a lop-sided woman?' and, 'They took my breast off me while I was asleep; can I believe them when they say they have removed all the tumour?' Ann had a very supportive family and general practitioner but she found that it took her almost a year before she felt sufficiently confident in herself as a person to go dancing or swimming without the fear that her 'secret' would be disclosed.

Ann's reaction is typical of many of the women who have to face having a breast removed. Apart from the actual loss of the breast, and the trauma and upset that many patients experience when undergoing surgery, there is the accompanying feeling of mutilation. The feeling of mutilation may be expressed as a loss of attractiveness or femininity. 'I feel that I am now only half a woman'. One's self-image has altered, with a consequent loss of wholeness, which can sometimes express itself as an upset or resentment of 'busty women' who may seem to be flaunting themselves in front of you. There may also be anger at television advertisements for bras.

In Ann's case she experienced an accompanying loss of opportunity for a normal relationship with a boyfriend or husband since she now saw herself as sexually undesirable. This reaction is one which is sometimes commented on by married women: 'How can I undress in front of my husband any more, I will put him off?' or 'The children always used to come into the bathroom when I was in the bath, but now I feel I want to lock the door and they'll wonder why'. A lot of unnecessary stress and suffering can be prevented if the husband, boyfriend or family can give a lot of reassurance about the acceptability of the patient after surgery. A sense of humour can go a long way towards easing the tensions, always providing that the jokes and comments do not become hurtful. Humour and sensitivity must go hand in hand.

The feelings of loss of femininity, and loss of self-image and attractiveness to others, are usually further complicated by the fears of malignancy and the frequent searching of the other breast for lumps. With the passage of time this eases, but in the early days patients will sometimes not wish to consider or discuss prostheses on the grounds that, 'there is no point. I shall not live long enough to wear them'.

When it is possible to prepare the patient for mastectomy before the operation it does seem to help if they can air some of their fears and anxieties about malignancy, about their appearance, and about the various cosmetic aids available. Talking to other people who have satisfactorily readjusted after a mastectomy can also be of benefit and is one of the advantages of a link with the *Mastectomy Association*. People will react in different ways to any surgical procedure, but it is helpful in the preoperative contact to try to assess the needs and difficulties that each patient may experience both during and after the operation. I feel it is helpful to include the husband as far as possible because the loss of the breast can become the crisis point which leads to breakdown rather than growth in a marriage that is already under strain. The extent of the grief reaction following mastectomy seems to be related to the importance the patient and family place on bosoms, and the extent to which the patient is reassured that she is still a worthwhile person. The husband can be a key figure in providing this reassurance. A study in Oxford[1] has shown that many of the women who were surveyed following a mastectomy mourned the loss of the breast during the ensuing year, and here again one finds parallels with the process of grief following a death.

The initial stage of shock and disbelief is usually brought on by the discovery of a lump. This gives way to a growing awareness of the true nature of the diagnosis, which can be thrust upon the person if they suddenly find that the breast has been removed. Telling them it might be does not always mean they accept the fact that it will be removed. The mixture of feelings which may be experienced can vary from relief that the growth has been removed, to resentment at being mutilated. This may be expressed as resentment of the hospital and the family for allowing it to happen.

As many mastectomy patients are only in hospital for a short while (7 to 10 days) the hospital staff may not see the patient

[1] Maguire (1976) p. 35.

and family for long enough to see their various reactions after the first few days. It is often the general practitioner and the prosthesis fitter who will see the patient long-term. The trauma of mastectomy may be eased by skilful counselling by the surgeon, ward sister, G.P., physiotherapist, prosthesis fitter and family all playing their part both before and after the operation.

This sort of guidance implies a reasonable amount of knowledge on the part of those caring for the patient, and it would seem that this is not always available. While many of the nurses surveyed in a Welsh hospital placed mastectomy in a high emotional disturbance group, together with colostomy, hysterectomy and below-knee amputation, there seemed to be a lack of knowledge of the patient's problems and the advice she would need.

The main problem appeared to be a lack of information given to the patient regarding procedures, postoperative symptoms and apparatus, and prostheses, as well as a discussion with the appliance officer and the Mastectomy Association. Additional information should be made available in the form of leaflets for patients to read at their leisure.

From the study, it was felt that some of the nurses should have special training and hence advise patients in this specialist area. They should be able to assess the social, psychological and physical state of the women and their husbands, and provide advice and re-assurance.[1]

The formation of a *Mastectomy Association* in 1973 is an encouraging development in that they can do much to help and encourage the patient, family and staff who are involved in the rehabilitative process. This of course, already happens with the organizations which offer support to patients who have had a colostomy, ileostomy or an amputation. Full details of the

[1] Jones (1977) p. 559.

information that patients and staff find helpful is included in a recently published book which has a very practical and human approach, well illustrated with personal accounts by various people who have had the operation.[1]

The male patient

It is usual to assume that the term 'mastectomy' only refers to female patients. Although carcinoma of the male breast is rare, when it does occur it can cause not only alarm, but also considerable embarrassment to the patient.

A 52-year-old man discovered a small lump under the nipple of his right breast. He ignored it for two months and then, when it failed to disappear, he consulted his family doctor. He was referred to the local hospital where he subsequently was admitted for surgery. The growth was found to be malignant and the surgeon performed a mastectomy, removing as much of the breast tissue and surrounding tissues as he could, and referred the patient for radiotherapy. The patient's reactions to his condition were similar to those described by female patients: the denial of symptoms and the hope that it would go away; the feeling of 'why me?'; the fear of malignancy; and periods of depression and withdrawal. However, there was for this patient an added source of discomfort. When he attended the radiotherapy centre (some 50 miles from his home) he found that he had to sit in a queue of ladies all attending for similar treatment and breast problems. From the beginning he had found it difficult to acknowledge that he had 'breast trouble' as this seemed to imply a threat to his masculinity. To be asked to attend for treatment at what seemed to be a women's clinic only added insult to injury and he suffered considerable upset and embarrassment which he felt unable to express to the staff. He told me that he had no complaints about his treatment as such, only about the

[1] Robinson & Swash (1977).

management of himself as a person. In spite of his treatment, the tumour soon invaded the pectoral muscles and eventually the bones. He died two years after the first appearance of the 'lump'.

A similar embarrassment was experienced by the male author of an article in a women's magazine, where he described his experience of having to attend 'The Breast Clinic' for the examination of a lump in his breast—which subsequently turned out to be caused by mastitis.

'I'll have to fill in some forms. Name, address, religion, G.P.'s name, next of kin, etc., etc., etc.' She entered these details on two forms, the outside of an envelope, the inside of a file and on an appointments card. Meanwhile the queue behind me was reaching alarming proportions as the halt and the lame turned up for their afternoon sort out. People were ranged up on both sides of me at the desk, and as the clerk annotated each of my documents with the words 'The Breast Clinic' in prominent blue felt tip, I was aware of the stares of the curious, and a slowly growing silence.

As a finale, and to make sure that everyone knew of my predicament, she handed me the whole collection of papers, then leaned over the desk, and said in a voice which must have carried to Streatham, 'The breast clinic is up the stairs to the right.' The crowd respectfully parted and I fled, feeling that my right breast must now look like one half of a badly balanced 40C cup.

I surmounted the stairs, turned right, and from nowhere a phalanx of nurses converged on me. 'Men's surgical is the other way,' said the leader, a formidable upper ranker.

'I have an appointment at the breast clinic,' I said. Stunned silence. 'Where's your letter?'

I produced it. Looking incredulous and defeated, she took it away to return a few minutes later, smirking. 'You'd better take your coat off and get on the scales.' I complied. 'Now sit over there.'

I took my place, feeling like a bacon sandwich at a Jewish wedding, among a variegated collection of the fairer sex, several of whom were in a state of *semi-déshabillé*. I looked around at the decorations, mostly posters urging me to have a cervical smear, check my breasts regularly for lumps and not to be embarrassed about having a check-up for V.D. It was obvious, after a few minutes, that my intrusion into this last bastion of womanhood short of the maternity ward was something of a strain to all concerned. To cut it short, I was summoned next.[1]

Although male breast lesions are rare one hopes that, when male patients are referred for examination and treatment, the understanding of the staff whom they meet will minimize the embarrassment and thus prevent situations similar to those just quoted.

The Stoma Patient

'I would rather be dead than like this.' This comment was made by a 50-year-old lady who had looked at her colostomy for the first time. She later asked, 'How can I face people knowing that my anus now sticks out at the front? They will smell me coming a mile away.' The loss of normal function and dignity occasioned by the formation of a stoma, together with the fear of detection, can be a daunting problem for many patients and families.

The ability to control the bladder or the bowel is a very important step in the development of the child. This is evident when talking to most mothers with toddlers, who see the end of nappies as a great milestone. To lose this ability has far-reaching effects on the adult patient or the adolescent. This fact has only recently been referred to in medical and nursing textbooks on the care of surgical patients. A survey conducted in Southend and London in 1970[2] showed that 25% of colostomy patients contacted were depressed to the extent of needing medical treatment, and 50% were more socially isolated than the average person in the community. A subsequent survey

[1] Doak (1976).   [2] Devlin et al. (1971) p. 413.

conducted in 1973 in Manchester[1] showed similar findings with important social problems occurring in a significant proportion of patients who have had an abdominoperineal resection. These problems included lack of amenities such as an indoor toilet; difficulty with their appliance, its supply and disposal; problems with diet; problems relating to their work, home and social life. The loss experienced has many facets.

The experience and reaction to the loss

'We know what we are, but know not what we may be.'[2] One of the main problems for stoma patients is that, as they look at the stoma, they see very clearly what they have become. However, this perception of themselves can frequently make it difficult for them to accept what they *can* become if they can cope with their various forms of loss in a creative way.

Shock and revulsion. The first reaction for many patients when they see their stoma is one of revulsion and a feeling of mutilation. The patient may be very quiet and withdrawn and want nothing to do with the stoma, thus leaving it all to the nurse. This stage is very similar to that of 'shock and disbelief' in normal grieving.[3] The patient may show signs of a reactive depression and will watch the reactions of other people as they view the stoma. If the doctor, nurse, family or other patients, show any signs of disgust it will reinforce the patient's perception of himself as a stigmatized person. As a chaplain I am sometimes shown the stoma by patients because they wish to see my reaction to its appearance and working. The inability to accept the permanence of the stoma is sometimes indicated by the question 'When will it heal over?' or the comment 'I feel so dirty handling my own waste, it seems so unnatural'. This latter comment frequently comes from people who have always

[1] Sellwood (1974).   [2] Shakespeare, *Hamlet*, Act IV, scene v.
[3] See Ch. 1.

found toilet habits distasteful and have never come to terms with their own anatomy and bodily functions. There are, of course, others who take a delight in discussing their bowel habits with anyone who will listen! Another aspect of this period of shock and disbelief is the phenomenon of 'phantom rectum' where the patient may experience the desire to pass flatus or faeces by the normal route.

... in a special enquiry amongst 50 persons who had had complete rectal excision between 6 months and 14 years previously, Farley and Smith (1968) found that no less than 34 (68%) admitted to such symptoms... In another survey Devlin et al. (1971) put the incidence of phantom rectum at 50% of patients after rectal excision. The cause of the condition is unknown. In some cases the symptoms improve spontaneously over the years, in others there is no change. No treatment seems indicated beyond firm reassurance.[1]

Whilst the cause of this condition may not be known it seems reasonable to postulate that there may be similarities with the experience of amputees who may describe sensation in the limb that has been removed, and thus it may be a further manifestation of the person trying to adjust to life without the function, object or person. The bereaved also talk of times when they see or hear the deceased very near to them.[2]

Growing awareness. As the reality of having a stoma gradually sinks in, the patient will become more aware of its working and may express fears of smell, accident and giving offence to others. The fact that the patient is not able to control the expulsion of faeces and flatus seems to lead to later problems of social isolation and loss of dignity and acceptability to others. This is inter-related with the fear of detection and smell.

Many patients do not realize that the stoma is a sphincterless

[1] Goligher (1975) p. 734.   [2] See Ch. 1.

opening and that one cannot guarantee them a regular pattern of bowel movement. In fact one of the main aims of management of the patient is to enable him or her to cope with an incontinent anus with the minimum of soiling and inconvenience. Some patients are lucky that their stoma functions only once or twice a day at fairly predictable times, but one cannot claim that they 'have controlled it'. It is important from an early stage that the stoma appliance should be leak-proof and odour-proof if possible, so that the patient does not become too demoralized in the early stages. Much reassurance will be needed if there is an accidental spillage, since this can serve to confirm the patient's image of himself as dirty. This is especially relevant if the patient already has a disability which makes the physical handling of the appliance difficult, such as partial-sight, hemiplegia or arthritis.

In the film *'It's a Bit Different from This Time Last Year'* the patient portrayed is a middle-aged woman who has had a colostomy.[1] Following a period of withdrawal she eventually expresses her feelings of shame and guilt because she sees herself as unclean and unpleasant. She also asks whether her husband will want to touch her any more. The film shows the effect that the colostomy has upon her family life, especially upon the children. Basically, it is the problem of smell that they cannot cope with and it is eventually overcome by a change of appliance and the use of deodorant. A year later we see her at her birthday party, and we are shown how she has now readjusted to a normal way of life with her family.

The feeling of shame that some patients have can lead to them asking to have no visitors, or only the immediate family, because they cannot face others knowing. When they go home they may also become a recluse and be afraid to go out. After the first few days the fluid consistency of the faecal matter in the colostomy becomes firmer and more formed, and in many ways

[1] This film was made for Abbott Laboratories, Kent and was awarded the British Medical Association Gold Award in 1975.

this can be less acceptable to the patient. The patient may then feel happier with an opaque bag, and may need to be encouraged to experiment with diet.

Sometimes the patient will find the stoma so unacceptable that he or she will cease to care for it and will present in the doctor's surgery with a variety of skin problems. This seems to parallel the behaviour of the grieving widow or widower who ceases to care for themselves, even in matters of basic hygiene. It is difficult to know why apparently capable people preoperatively do not seem to manage very well afterwards, but one can postulate that perhaps they are saying to themselves, 'If it all goes wrong, and I show that I cannot manage it, they will have to put it back!'

In contrast to the colostomy patient, the person who has an ileostomy is frequently young and, for a woman especially, the feeling of disfigurement can be very strong. A young female patient may also ask about childbearing, sexual relationships and boyfriends and perhaps imagine that the stoma implies loss of fulfilment in this aspect of life. It often helps to link the patient with the *Ileostomy Association* where he or she can discuss these problems with others who have not found the ileostomy to be a barrier. Some patients have found that the general improvement in their health has, in fact, led to an overall improvement in their relationships.

Disturbance and loss of sexual function in the male arising from damage to the pelvic autonomic nerves is a common complication, especially in the older age groups.[1] The extent of the loss varies, with the extent of the pelvic dissection, from failure to ejaculate to impotence. In some cases this has led to subsequent marital breakdown. Because of the younger age group involved the problem can be more acute for the ileostomy patient, and this matter should certainly be discussed frankly with the patient before surgery. An even more difficult problem can arise with the male homosexual patient which he may feel unable to discuss with anyone. In effect, rectal excisional surgery

[1] Goligher (1975) p. 759.

in these circumstances can be disastrous and in two patients is known to have precipitated suicide.[1] Considerable understanding is needed if such patients are to cope with their special form of loss, anxiety and grief.

Compared with the colostomy patient, the ileostomist has frequently been chronically sick for many years and the operation may be seen as a way of gaining an improvement in health and independence. The younger age group also tends to mean greater adaptability. For the colostomy patient it often emerges that the shock of requiring a stoma is greater because 'I thought it was only my piles, doctor. Why did you need to do such drastic things to me?' To their way of perceiving things they have been made worse, not better. As with normal grieving, this question may also be expressed as 'Why should God let it happen to me?'[2]

In the case of the patient who has a urinary diversion stoma, the problems and sense of loss may be similar to those of other stoma patients. However, if the patient is a child there may be additional difficulties in that it is not a once-and-for-all adaptation. As the child grows up, both the parents and the child may have to re-adapt to a series of crises such as the repeated periods spent in hospital in the case of a spina bifida child; the failed aspirations; the transfer to a special school in some instances, and again at school-leaving age. The reaction of the parents to loss, such as guilt, resentment or over-protection may still be present (as a form of unresolved grief) and may be projected onto the hospital, the school and sometimes the child. The G.P. and the various support services would seem to have a vital role to play in listening to, and visiting, the family (as with all stoma patients). To help the parents is to help the child. In addition to the statutory services the local clergy should be a useful link between the family and neighbourhood support.

It is clear, from talking to many patients who have a stoma, and staff who have cared for them, that the creation of a stoma

[1] Devlin (1973).   [2] See Ch. 1.

is seen as a mutilation. It also gives rise to reactions very similar to those normally designated as 'grief'. The reaction of the patient to such mutilation will vary from one person to another, but is related to the care that they receive before the operation, whenever this has been possible. Such care is essentially a team approach with surgeon, ward staff, stoma therapist (where appointed) chaplain, patient, family and other 'adjusted' stoma patients each playing their part. Many writers place the responsibility for co-ordinating this care onto the surgeon:

Any surgeon contemplating the creation of a permanent colostomy or ileostomy must accept that he is going to be personally responsible for the preparation, operation, subsequent follow-up and, in co-operation with the general practitioner, for the support of the patient for the remainder of that individual's life.[1]

This responsibility is mainly in respect of the siting of the stoma, the choice of appliance, and the building of a relationship of trust which will enable the recognition and prompt dealing with any problems that arise.

Face and Neck

Mutilation resulting from injury

A patient who has received mutilating injuries as a result of a car accident, a fire or a bomb blast, may require quite extensive reconstructive surgery if some semblance of normality is to be restored. From the time of the injury, until any reconstructive surgery is completed, there can be considerable trauma for all concerned. There may be various aspects of loss ranging from

[1] Oates (1973) p. 3.

lack of acceptability to others, because of visual appearance, to probable loss of life. Any surgery that is undertaken is often viewed by patient and family with the hope that it will be the means of either restoring, or improving upon, the patient's former visual attractiveness. If such expectations are false there can be a further sense of loss as the patient and family try to accept the limitations of what can be done. This can sometimes rekindle any feelings of guilt or bitterness that may earlier have been associated with the cause of the injury. Staff are not immune to such feelings themselves, as indicated earlier,[1] and this can be an important factor to consider in the event of a major disaster and the needs of relief workers and staff.[2]

Mutilation as a result of surgery

For some patients the mutilation that they experience is not caused by accidental injury, but as a stage in an operation or treatment procedure. The impact of the loss that is experienced will depend upon the nature of the operation, how well the patient is prepared for the operation and the postoperative period, and the support of the family and staff.

Bill was aged 66 years when he first went to see his doctor because of a lump in his throat which made it difficult to eat, and to swallow. He was also losing weight. After various tests he was referred for radiotherapy and this led to a marked improvement. Four months later there was a recurrence of symptoms and he was referred for surgery. Bill's voice was also becoming more hoarse and it was decided that he had a tumour of the lower pharynx and that the larynx was also now involved. The implications of a pharyngectomy and laryngectomy were explained to Bill and his wife, but he felt the operation was worth it, if it led to relief of pain and an improvement in his

[1] See Ch. 3.   [2] Edwards (1976) p. 946.

health. After operation he made the following comment on some of his reactions:

I was worried about the operation and the thought of losing my voice, but was resigned it had to be done. It was a big shock later to be so weak and helpless and unable to call out for help. The nurses were very good, but of course they had other patients to deal with and I felt neglected. I was down the passage in a four-bedded side ward on my own (because of the infection). The nurses were going past all the time and would sometimes wave to me, or call out, but I could not call out to them. They would not stand in the doorway for long enough for me to show them I wanted to tell (or, more accurately, write) them something. Having a tube in my neck and being unable to talk was both frightening and frustrating. I felt helpless, isolated and neglected. I had two shocks. My voice had gone and, although nobody talked about it much, I believed that I was not cured. I think it was the sadness in people's eyes which made me think 'I have lost my voice for nothing.'

Bill still finds it difficult to accept the loss of his voice. He has to write down most of what he has to say and he finds that many of his visitors show impatience after a while and restrict the length of their visits. He has a vibrator on loan at present but is unable to use it, because the radiotherapy has affected the healing properties of his skin and his neck is very sore. It is therefore very painful for him to use the vibrator to aid his speech. He does, however, see it as a useful aid once his neck is less tender.

The loss of normal communication between husband and wife can also be a strain to the wife. The wife of a patient who had a carcinoma of the tongue found that he was unable to speak because of the insertion of irradiated needles.[1] An additional loss

[1] For clinical details on this procedure see Fish (1974) p. 170, and Capra (1972) p. 67.

was the lack of privacy on the ward which made it difficult for her to say and do things to reassure her husband of her continuing love and support. In spite of these difficulties they devised, and became proficient at communication by facial expression, touch and sign language, and by the use of a writing pad. They also plucked up courage to draw the curtains a little way around the bed when visiting. Initially, staff were ambivalent in their feelings towards this couple, but gradually they began to see that the wife was able to obtain information from the husband that they could not, and this led them also to explore other means of communication. After the needles had been removed, and the patient discharged, the husband and wife told me that what had initially been a sense of loss had ultimately proved to be a gain, for they had grown closer together during this experience of exploring other forms of communication. They had rediscovered the importance of *listening* and of just *being* present, as well as speaking.

If the patient has had to have part of a jaw removed the intermediate stages between admission and discharge can sometimes be upsetting for the relatives, and this can be transmitted to the patient. One patient who had cancer of the lower jaw received radiotherapy in the first instance. This was followed by a very extensive operation which led to a profound sense of shock and mutilation. When I discussed these reactions with him he was full of praise for the surgeon and explained how carefully the surgeon had prepared him for the operation. He explained how frustrating he found it to be unable to talk in the early stages, although he knew that this was only temporary. When his son came to visit him, on the second day after his operation, he had to dash out of the ward and was heard to be sick in the corridor. The patient was very distressed by this, for at that time he had not seen what he looked like as mirrors were not allowed. It was this incident which brought home to the patient the extent of his loss. He thought that if his own son could not face seeing him then what about the outside world? The son felt very guilty for reacting the way he did and the ward staff were able to reconcile father and son and to point out that this was a transition stage in the father's treatment. They also assured both that the end result would be a great improvement. Having met this patient subsequently, the only indication that there has been major surgery to the face, is a patch of scar tissue on the forehead which, as the patient remarked, 'doesn't show when I've got my hat on'.

Much of what has been said above in connection with tumours of the face and neck can also be applied to patients admitted for neurosurgery. Here they may experience similar forms of loss, which will usually start with the loss of their hair.

Ophthalmic surgery

A further surgical area where there may be associated loss is ophthalmic surgery. Enucleation of an eye involves the removal of the eyeball and is undertaken for the following reasons:

A blind, painful eye.
An eye which constitutes a danger to the patient's health, for example when there is a possibility of a malignant tumour metastasizing.
An eye which has been injured so extensively that repair is impossible, or where there is a risk of the damaged eye causing sympathetic ophthalmia in its undamaged fellow.[1]

The removal of an eye, even if the patient acknowledges that it is diseased, is always a great shock and requires great understanding and reassurance. The need for the operation may not be accepted by the patient if there have been no distressing symptoms, and this can lead to requests for second and third opinions.

As with the patient who has been advised of the need for a

---

[1] Darling & Thorpe (1975) p. 181.

stoma or a mastectomy, the patient who is to have an eye removed requires time to come to terms with the loss. During this time the patient needs to feel able to express fears and to ask questions about artificial eyes and their ease of fitting and appearance. He or she may also wish to express concern about the other eye and the possibility of total loss of vision. The wider subject of blindness has been very helpfully and briefly described in *Ophthalmic Nursing*, and the reader is referred to this book for further details.[1]

Amputation

One of the more obvious forms of loss, resulting from surgery, is that which follows the amputation of a limb. Most staff would agree that patients who have to have a limb amputated are going to experience both psychological and social problems. However, much depends on the experience and insight of the staff as to how far they recognize and cope with some of the needs and problems of the patient. To say that Fred is 'depressed' after his operation can imply a short term and transitory problem. To say that Fred is 'grieving' over the loss of his right arm, which would include periods of depression, is to imply the need for a much longer time scale for his readjustment.

The problems experienced by the patient will clearly depend on the limb that is lost, the extent of the amputation, and the patient's reaction to previous experiences of loss in his life. The disability may, therefore, range from complete immobility to the need 'to acquire' new skills and a new life style with an artificial limb. Some patients seem able to cope with this very well and their rehabilitation progresses very smoothly. However, there are patients who have to 'unlearn' many things and for whom readjustment is a long and painful process which may never be completed.

[1] *Ibid.* pp. 186–91.

Fred was admitted to hospital with gangrene of the right leg at the age of 60 years. Following a discussion with Fred and his wife it was decided to perform a below knee amputation. Fred had had a great deal of pain and because of this he not only agreed to the operation, but he almost begged the surgeon to remove his leg. After the operation he made good progress, but a few days later he became very withdrawn. He received anti-depressant therapy and, although he did appear brighter, he still seemed to be fretting. The staff nurse had formed a good relationship with him and eventually he disclosed to her that he was dreading the artificial leg that he had heard he might receive. 'I've seen the tin legs they gave my mates after the war and I don't want one of them. I'd rather stay like Long John Silver than be clanking around everywhere'. The staff nurse explained that modern limbs were greatly improved and that he would be amazed when he saw them at the limb-fitting centre. She also asked Fred if he remembered the barber who visited the ward, and then informed Fred that he had an artificial leg. The process of sharing his grief and his misconception had begun. Later that year Fred revisited the ward and told the staff how pleased he was with his new mobility and that he was willing to visit anyone else who seemed to be apprehensive about life with a new limb.

In one of the earlier studies into the reactions of patients to the amputation of a limb a parallel with grief was shown.[1] In that study reference was made to the fact that a part of one's body had been irrevocably lost and that the patient would no longer feel a whole man. It was suggested that this reaction had to be anticipated and recognized if the patient was to be spared a psychic trauma more disabling than the amputation itself.

A more recent study has compared the reactions of 21 widows and 46 amputees to their experience of loss, all of whom were around 50 years of age.[2] The people interviewed were seen 4 to 8 weeks and again 13 months after the bereavement or

[1] Kessler (1951) pp. 107–8.   [2] Parkes (1975) pp. 204–10.

operation. They were nearly all seen in their own home and lived in the London boroughs.

Initial reaction. It was found that about 50% of both groups experienced a sense of numbness and inability to accept the loss as having happened. Gradually this numbness wore off and the widow began to pine for her lost husband, and this was a very painful and tearful time. In contrast, the amputee only occasionally pined for the amputated limb. More usually the amputee mourned the loss of the life style and activities that had been lost along with the limb. These included the job, workmates, sporting activities and any other activity which was thought to require the presence of sound limbs. This was borne out for me by a 75-year-old man who had been a footballer in earlier life. He played his last game at 55 years. However, following the amputation of his left leg (his goal scoring leg) he complained bitterly that he would no longer be able to play football!

Four to eight weeks later. At this stage it was found that there were many familiar features of grief, such as a preoccupation with thoughts of the loss, avoidance of reminders, and clear visual memories of the lost object. These reactions were more common in the bereaved group. However, the amputee group reported a sense of presence of the lost limb more frequently (89%) than the widowed group reported the sense of presence of the lost spouse (28%). Pining, bitterness and depression alternated, and frequently both groups showed a strong preoccupation with thoughts of the lost limb or person, sometimes with clear visual images. This study also showed a distinction between visualizing the lost object in the mind's eye and a strong sense of its physical presence. This phenomenon has been described as 'phantom limb', which was reported by the majority of the amputees interviewed, and paralleled by many of the widows.

Thirteen months after the loss. At this stage many of the differences between the amputees and the widows had disappeared. The prevalence of such features as tearfulness, tension, irritability, anorexia and avoidance of reminders had fallen in the bereaved group, while remaining virtually unchanged in the amputee group. This resulted in a closer similarity of reaction in the two groups at this stage. The one exception was the persistence of the sense of the presence of the lost object, which remained in 56% of the amputee group and only 14% of the bereaved group.

The study points out that getting a job is often an important turning point for the bereaved. However, 13 months after amputation only a third of the amputees compared with two thirds of the widows were working satisfactorily. The amputees had been hampered in this by persisting physical disability, lack of confidence and an unwillingness on the part of employers to accept older amputees. It was not very surprising that these experiences led the amputee group to be more preoccupied with their loss.

In his discussion of the study, Parkes indicates that there is a process of realization in which the individual has slowly and painfully to reassess his new relationship to the world as it really is, and to reconstruct a new world view. Although the amputee may not feel impelled to cry and to search for the lost limb he certainly expresses sorrow for his situation. This sorrow implies a pining, not so much for the limb itself, as for the world view and his or her role in the world, which has now been lost. This is clearly linked with the concept of body image referred to earlier.[1]

One of the major problems for the amputee is that he or she may experience a number of raised hopes and disappointments, with amputation as the culmination. The difficulties of rehabilitation and reintegration into society account for some of the differences in the two groups. The other main difference is

[1] See p. 54.

that concerning the persistence of a sense of the physical presence of the lost limb and the phenomenon of 'phantom limb'. Overall, the study shows a close parallel between the reaction of the amputee group and the widowed group to their respective losses, and the relevance of the terms 'grief' and 'mourning' to their reactions.

Phantom limb

Alterations in body image can lead to an experience of a phantom limb whereby the patient may be convinced that the body has not been altered by the operation. A patient will sometimes ask, 'Why have you not removed my leg?' in the early postoperative period. A woman recovering from child-birth may sometimes find it hard to believe the child is born, and that she is no longer pregnant, in spite of the gradual reduction in size of the abdomen and the fact that she can now see her feet.

Immediately following amputation the patient frequently experiences sensation in the absent limb, especially in the distal part. The sensation may vary from a 'tingling' feeling to 'pain'. This sensation gradually diminishes for most patients but for some it can take several years. If the mourning process for the loss is unresolved for some reason, the symptoms may persist and will affect the rehabilitation. The problems created by this can give the patient a reason to withdraw from responsibilities and to remain the focus of medical and family attention. Guilt, feelings of uselessness and unresolved grief are frequently found to be associated with persistent phantom limb.[1]

Conclusion

Objectively, a loss may seem to be the same for several patients, but the significance of that loss will vary from person to person. Loss of self-esteem is a very basic loss. Because self-esteem is

[1] Kolb (1954); Parkes (1973) pp. 97–108.

built up by family members and a wide variety of other people, they will have an important part to play in the rehabilitation of the patient. The attitudes of staff towards disfigurement and surgical loss will also shape the patient's reaction and that of the family. It is not unusual to find that a patient who has done well in hospital regresses when he or she returns home, because the family are not psychologically prepared to continue the re-habilitation. Much falls to the general practitioner and the community services to educate the family to cope.[1] The close family need to be part of the caring team from the moment of admission to the time of discharge. However, one has to ack-nowledge that while some families will come to assist the patient to recovery, others will come to be patients alongside the patient!

If the patient is not able to reorganize his or her body image the resulting emotional problems may require psychiatric help. People who are disfigured, for whatever reason, frequently suffer stigmatization in a society which places great emphasis on appearance. Advertisements frequently imply the 'best' people are those who are young, healthy and whole. Consequently the disfigured can become objects of pity, fear or revulsion, according to the observer's own anxiety and phantasy about deformity.[2] Such stigmatization can perhaps be interpreted as 'the price to be paid' by the person who is disfigured for infringing the norms of society. If the patient enjoys secure and loving relationships in which he or she knows that it is not physical appearance, ability or prowess that is the reason for the relationship then he or she will be more able to resolve the feelings generated by the loss. It is in the context of a loving, accepting relationship that we all may learn to accept that we are accepted though unacceptable.[3]

Summary

The impact of the loss of a part of the body following surgery, or the loss of appearance through facial disfigurement, is closely

[1] Keywood (1977) p. 66 ff.   [2] Goffman (1968) p. 162.   [3] Tillich (1965) p. 160.

related to the way in which the person feels about himself. It is also dependent upon the relationships between the patient, family, and those caring for them.

In the cases of mastectomy, amputation of limbs, and the creation of a stoma, the importance of anticipatory guidance is stressed. Ideally there should be good communication between all concerned as to what will happen, why, and the postoperative period and rehabilitation help. The period of readjustment to the loss will be much longer than the time spent in hospital and, drawing on the parallel of bereavement, may be as long as 18 months to 2 years. The patient who undergoes mutilating surgery of the face also shows a similar reaction to grief which, if for a malignant tumour, may be superimposed with anticipatory grief for a possible loss of his or her own life.

Anticipatory preparation can enable the person to begin building up a realistic picture of the new world view before the old is destroyed. It may also help to introduce the patient to others who have faced a similar loss and who have readjusted to it. In this way the patient may come to see some of the new opportunities that may be open to him or her after recovery from the initial surgery.

It must be acknowleged that *some* patients will cope very well with such surgical loss, as with previous forms of loss in their life, and hence may not manifest any grief-like reaction.

References and Further Reading

Boore, J. R. P. (1977) Preoperative care of patients. *Nursing Times*, March 24, pp. 409–11.

Capra, L. G. (1972) *The Care of the Cancer Patient*. London: Heinemann Medical.

Darling, V. & Thorpe, M. (1975) *Ophthalmic Nursing*. London: Baillière Tindall.

Devlin, H. B., Plant, J. A. & Griffin, M. (1971) Aftermath of surgery for anorectal cancer. *Br. med. J., iii,* 413.

Devlin, H. B. (1973) Stoma care—the quality of life. *Stoma Care*. Queensborough: Abbott Laboratories.

Doak, N. (1976) We're a couple of swells. *She*, February, pp. 40–1.

Edwards, J. G. (1976) Psychiatric aspects of civilian disasters. *Br. med. J., i*, 944–7.

Fish, E. J. (1974) *Surgical Nursing*. London: Baillière Tindall.

Goffman, E. (1968) *Stigma*. Harmondsworth: Penguin.

Goligher, J. C. (1975) *Surgery of the Anus, Rectum and Colon*. London: Baillière Tindall.

Jones, M. (1977) Mastectomy. *Nursing Times*, April 21, p. 559.

Kessler, H. H. (1951) Psychological preparation of the amputee. *Ind. Med. Surg., 20*, 107–8.

Keywood, O. (1977) *Nursing in the Community*. London: Baillière Tindall.

Kolb, L. C. (1954) *The Painful Phantom*. Springfield, Illinois, U.S.A.: C. C Thomas.

Maguire, P. & Hampson, M. (1976) The operation was successful but the patient wants to die... *Wld. Med.*, Nov. 3, pp. 35–7.

Oates, G. D. (1973) Colostomy and ileostomy. *Stoma Care*. Queensborough: Abbott Laboratories.

Parkes, C. M. (1973) Factors determining the persistence of phantom pain in the amputee. *J. psychosom. Res. 17*, 97–108.

Parkes, C. M. (1975) Psycho-social transitions: comparison between reactions to loss of a limb and loss of a spouse. *Br. J. Psychiat. 127*, 204–10.

Robinson, N. & Swash, I (1977) *Mastectomy: A Patient's Guide to Coping with Breast Cancer*. Wellingborough, Northants: Thorsons.

Schilder, P. (1935) *The Image and Appearance of the Human Body*. London: Routledge & Kegan Paul.

Sellwood, R. A. (1974) Prognosis and rehabilitation of patients with cancer of the rectum and colon. *Stoma Surg. Rehabil.* Queensborough: Abbott Laboratories.

Smith, Jo Ann Kelley (1977) *Free Fall*. London: S.P.C.K. This book was written in the final months of her life and takes the reader through the events which followed her mastectomy and the realization that she had terminal cancer. She describes her emotional conflicts, and the questions which challenged her Christian faith, the effect on her family and the support she required.

Spraggon, E. M. (1975) *Urinary Diversion Stomas*. Edinburgh: Churchill Livingstone. This is written in a simple straightforward manner both to help patients who have to adjust to living with a urinary stoma and to help them live a full and satisfying life.

Symposium on Stoma Care (1976) *Nursing Times*, January 8. This covers literature from the various manufacturers of prostheses and appliances.

Tillich, P. (1965) *The Courage to Be*. London: Fontana Library, Collins.

Wright, B. A. (1960) *Physical Disability—A Psychological Approach*. New York: Harper and Row.

6 General Medicine

Tradition and convenience have led to the care of the sick being divided into various classes, based largely on either the part of the body affected or on the type of treatment involved. Medicine, as opposed to surgery, is accordingly concerned with people whose illness is largely that of disordered function (such as cardiac, respiratory, neurological or endocrine disorders) together with those disorders where there may be degenerative change. However, there is no sharp dividing line between those requiring medical and surgical treatment and often both may be employed at different stages of disease.[1]

When a person becomes ill, whether it is because of a common cold or something more serious, the illness often brings with it a variety of restrictions, symptoms and limitations which the patient will usually accept. This is because the patient expects some discomfort and disturbance of life style, but he or she anticipates that this will only be temporary. If it becomes clear that the illness is likely to continue indefinitely, and the patient will become chronically sick, then the losses hitherto accepted now assume a new significance because of their probable permanent nature.

The response of the patient to this new realization will vary and depend upon the nature of the illness, the support available,

[1] Chapman (1977) p. 1.

and the previously formed personality and the personal ability to cope. A period of mourning may ensue while the person tries to adjust to the actual or impending losses. Because of other more prominent features of the particular illness, the grief and mourning may not always be recognized as such. If they are recognized or suspected then those caring for the patient may try to ignore them because of the feelings of inadequacy that they may arouse.

The care of someone who is chronically ill will make different demands from the care of someone who is acutely ill. The treatment of acute sickness, which leads to cure, can be very rewarding. There may be very little evidence or experience of loss and, after the initial phase of the illness is over, the patient is either discharged from hospital or, if nursed at home,[1] starts to mobilize and resume normal activities. By contrast, the person who is chronically ill may experience many acute episodes, with possible admission to hospital, and those who are trying to treat and care have to come to terms with their own limitations and inability to cure, as well as the frustrations that this can create. Although it has now become something of a platitude, the distinction between *curing* and *caring* assumes particular importance in the care of the chronically ill person as already recognized with the terminally ill person. This implies a concern for the *person* which is wider that the eradication of a disease process, and which may contain the possibility of cure but does not cease once a cure is no longer attainable.[2]

One also has to distinguish between the *wants* and *needs* of the patient. The patient, obviously, *wants* a complete cure or complete relief from symptoms. Amongst the various *needs* of the patient will be the need for support in accepting the illness and any treatment that may be necessary, and the need to feel understood as a person who, come what may, will not be abandoned. The wants and the needs may be expressed in different ways to different people. The doctor may get a list of aches and pains or

---

[1] About 90% of all illness is cared for at home.   [2] Eardley (1977).

a 'much the same'. The district nurse may get a different list of complaints. The family may get complaints about not visiting often enough, or about the food. The priest may hear various confessions of guilt relating to unresolved quarrels or resentments. There is always the danger that one may be 'played off' against the other, and there needs to be a good relationship between them so that they may, without breaking confidences, co-operate in trying to meet the changing needs of the patient and prevent other forms of loss.

Age is an important aspect in the assessment of the loss element in an illness. A young child who has grown up knowing that there must be regular trips to a treatment centre, or receiving daily drug therapy, will have a different attitude from the adult who suddenly develops a chronic illness and sees the treatment as an unwarranted intrusion. This is not to say that a young child will not also become frustrated and rebellious. With the child who has a congenital heart defect there may be several restrictions which, if the symptoms are not too severe, may lead to conflict over whether you obey the doctors and your parents, or do you take the risk and join in the sports with your friends?

Sometimes the patient will become a veritable hypochondriac with every pain and symptom being noted, reported and worried about. This arises from focussing down on the main site of the illness and living, for example, in an 'ulcer-centred world'. A chest pain which would not worry a normally healthy person may raise great anxiety in someone who has had a previous myocardial infarction. Each incident like this serves to remind one of an impending loss that one has been trying to ignore or deny. There is a tendency for patients either to deny the illness exists, or to focus so much on what has been lost that the loss becomes distorted and may be perceived as much greater than it later turns out to have been.

The previous description[1] of the grief process as an initial reaction of *shock and disbelief* leading to a *growing awareness* and

[1] Ch. 1.

then *resolution*, showed the need for time and adequate support to enable this to happen. The person who has a long term illness or disability will also require time to learn to avoid or restrict various previous activities as well as to acquire new coping mechanisms. In both cases one needs support and help to set meaningful and realistic goals if a sense of personal worth is to be restored.

The loss experienced by the acutely ill person is usually only a temporary one. The chronically ill person may also experience acute phases, but the total experience of loss can frequently be greater than that of the acutely ill person. In this chapter, therefore, we shall focus mainly on some of the losses that may be experienced in connection with a *selection* of chronic conditions and disabilities.

Loss of Vision

Blindness may arise out of injury, as an accompaniment to another disease, or as a result of the ageing process. The onset of loss of vision may be gradual or sudden, and the resultant loss may be partial or total. In the event of sudden loss of vision the resultant shock can be enormous.

The initial reaction to loss of vision may render the person immobile, expressionless and depressed. The person may also be very preoccupied with the total dependency that they feel and the loss of individual freedom. This period of shock and depression is normal and parallels that described earlier in connection with normal grieving.

After the initial feeling of shock wears off, the normal, healthy individual will often be concerned with economic loss and loss of freedom. Feelings of disfigurement may also be expressed, because the person is now unsure what facial expressions or postures he is presenting to other people, since he or she is no longer able to 'read' this in the other person's face. It is at this stage that the blind person has to begin to accept a new body image, and any skills that can be learnt will greatly help to improve morale. The rehabilitation of the person who has experienced visual loss will aim at restoring as much independence as possible, and to help the person to be reintegrated into society, thus minimizing the experience of further losses. The extent to which this can be achieved will depend upon the willingness of the person to be rehabilitated, the age, and the extent of visual loss and accompanying disease.

One can think of many blind people who are very well adjusted to their disability. They are often very cheerful, active and happy, and others who meet them for the first time may not be aware that they are blind. One aspect of blindness, that is often commented upon, is the extent to which the other senses are often developed and the need to develop a good memory. The work of the various associations for the blind, and of the rehabilitation centres, is invaluable in supporting and encouraging independence as well as educating society of the needs of the visually handicapped. When caring for a person who is blind, introducing oneself by touch and by voice is very helpful. Accepting that blindness is not necessarily totally incapacitating can help to guard against an over-protective attitude that will ultimately restrict any freedom the blind person may already have.[1]

Failure to adjust to the loss of vision can lead to anxiety, withdrawal and dependence. The initial shock wears off, the person becomes more aware of what has been lost and anticipates other future losses as a result, and may become aggressive. This is paralleled by bereavement studies where the bereaved may stick at a particular point in the mourning process, such as the bitterness they feel at the death of the deceased. Some people who have experienced loss of vision may also remain very bitter and angry with themselves and those who are sighted and closest to them.

[1] Darling & Thorpe (1975) Ch. 16; Perks (1975).

A 45-year-old man went progressively blind over a three-year period. He resented his failing vision and blamed the hospital for it. He believed that the doctors who had treated him had caused him to lose his sight and now would not help him. He refused to stop driving until the day when he had an accident and severely damaged the car and a brick wall. Fortunately no-one was injured. He saw the loss of the car as the first step towards rendering him helpless, and when his sight eventually went altogether he felt very bitter. He became jealous of his wife's vision and started to accuse her of having an 'affair' with a neighbour. She had in fact sought, and received, support from the husband of a neighbour following her own husband's threats of violence and fits of temper. The blind husband refused the help of the welfare worker for the blind in that area, and he told his wife that he would commit suicide if she ever left him. One day she left work at 4.00 p.m. as usual, but missed her bus home. Because of this she was a quarter of an hour late arriving home. When she entered the house, she was shocked to find her husband dead on the kitchen floor, with the gas poker in his mouth. The husband had 'staged' the scene ready for her return, but he had not anticipated that she might miss the bus, and the whole idea had misfired. It took a long while for the wife to work through her own feelings of relief and guilt that resulted from her husband's death.

Loss of Hearing

Initially, loss of hearing may be limited to no longer being able to pick out what is happening in the background. Gradually this extends to an inability to comprehend everything that is being said to one. The process can be so gradual that the person is not really aware that it is happening. This can lead to accusations that others are always mumbling! As deafness progresses it can lead to feelings of isolation, dejection and distrust of those around. The fact that the loss may not be equally distributed across the frequencies accounts for situations where some deaf people hear only what others do not want them to hear.

The deafness that may accompany the normal ageing process may be denied or not recognized if the onset is gradual. Some people become quite angry if it is suggested that their hearing may not be as good as it used to be, since this infers they are ageing and they do not wish to acknowledge the fact.

This reluctance to acknowledge that we all must age, and accept the changes that will accompany ageing, is also reflected in the comment of a teenage girl to her grandmother following the grandmother's discharge from hospital. 'Do you know why I didn't come to visit you while you were in hospital? I just could not face seeing myself when I am old'.

The extent to which a person adjusts to loss of hearing depends upon individual personality, and it can become an obstacle to satisfactory personal and emotional adjustment. Reactions may range from denial and withdrawal to concentrating on other symptoms and the exploitation of the disability (or 'convenient deafness'). In rare cases the person may become psychiatrically disturbed and develop a paranoid state because of the belief that people are 'whispering' about them.

In the adult, since hearing has little effect on an already developed speech and mobility, one can expect a good re-adjustment to the loss of hearing. In the young child the results may depend upon the age at which the disability occurs and whether there are associated problems of speech development, school, and the formation of relationships with others. Just as one should not assume that blind people are automatically deaf (and therefore raise one's voice when speaking) so one should not assume that all deaf people will be dumb.

Chronic Bronchitis

Albert cried

He was 56 and it was 1958. He lived in a colliery house and we sat by a coal fire. Immediately upon my arrival 'mother' had been despatched to the kitchen to mash a pot of tea for t'mister.

I had been asked to visit by the Coal Board doctor who had examined Albert with regard to early retirement. Some matter related to benefit had seemed to need attention and here I was. The welfare matter was quickly dealt with, but as we waited for the tea we talked.

Albert had gone straight to the pit on leaving school and was working on the coal face at the age of 18. In the 1930s there was much unemployment among miners and he counted himself lucky to be in Yorkshire where there was work most days for the skilled miner. The coal was won with pick and shovel and the pay was poor. Poor though it was, it was better than the dole.

When machine mining and better wages began to come in the early 1950s, Albert was already experiencing difficulties with his breathing due to bronchitis. He began to have periods off sick every winter—two to three weeks at a time at first, 'just a bit of chestiness'. But eventually he was off work for two to three months at a time, which he very much resented, and in the hope of working more regularly he asked for lighter work. As he told me, the only thing light about the work whether on the underground haulage roads or on the surface was the money.

Soon he could work in the summer months only and now after 15 months continuous absence he would have to accept early retirement.

As we talked the fire burnt lower—it was still high by anyone but a miner's standards—and he made to reach for the coal bucket. The effort was too much for him and the tears ran down his face as he called for mother to 'come and mend t'fire'. I encouraged him to talk. He told me how sitting still he felt fine, but the least effort was too much for him. He, who had earned his living and supported his family by shovelling coal, couldn't even make the fire up.

He talked about life in the pits. He had carefully advised his sons against work in the pit—the dirt, the dark and the danger—the feeling of being different and despised by clean collar workers.

Nonetheless it was clear that he had gloried in the chance to use his strength to win coal, in the wonderful comradeship and inter-dependence of miners underground, the sense of belonging to a special breed of men. He had a special contempt for young miners who thought their work was hard—he'd had to get the coal by hand—they'd got machines to do it for them. There was more—his feelings towards the N.C.B., the Union and the doctors of the Medical Board who he felt had cheated him of a pension for pneumoconiosis. In my experience, most miners with bronchitis are convinced their disease is due to dusty conditions and therefore certifiable for compensation.

Now he belonged no more. His sickness benefit and social security payment did not enable him to call at the institute for a pint more than once a week, and pride forbade that he should go there hoping one of his mates would treat him. His concessionary coal had been cut from nine tons a year to five and he had to rely on his son to tend and race his pigeons. On his good days he would go to the loft and handle his birds, but never was he fit to clean out.

The tea had come and gone and my next call was due. I promised to call again, for I knew he had further need to talk through his problems.

In the late 1950s, five Yorkshire miners retired every week through ill health—four of those five through bronchitis. I saw Albert—who listened to the others?

During the talk between Albert and the social worker, it emerged that Albert had experienced a variety of losses as a result of his medical condition.

He had been a miner all his life and clearly took a great pride in what he did. To be a 'working man' was infinitely better than living on the dole. His periods of sickness were resented as indications that he was not as strong as he would wish to be. Physical fitness and strength were important qualities in his community and, in one way, his manhood was being threatened. When visiting elderly men I have often been struck by the pride taken in being able to say, 'This is my first illness in 60 years. I've never lost a day's work'. Therefore, in the early stages of his illness, Albert ignored the symptoms as far as possible, denied that he was ill and continued working. It was not until the symptoms became more severe that he went to the doctor and started having to have 'time off'.

Denial is a very common first reaction and often leads to the patients either not seeking treatment or treating themselves in some way. This is shown very clearly with patients who have a myocardial infarction and who may not accept that there is anything wrong with them, thus refusing to rest or accept treat-ment. Previous experience also affects a person's reaction. Patients who have had no previous knowledge of heart disease may have little anxiety and set themselves to regulating their diet and activity, and to learning about their condition. By con-trast, patients who know of relatives who have died at an early age with the same symptoms, may be rigid with fear and unwilling to move a muscle. They may not share their reasons for this behaviour with anyone and just become progressively more withdrawn from reality. Albert denied his illness, in the early stages, because he had seen what had happened to other miners and so he knew what sort of life would lie ahead of him if he admitted defeat now.

Eventually Albert had to seek lighter work away from the coal face. This was a further blow to his pocket and his pride. As his condition worsened he had to accept an early retirement on the grounds of ill health—with accompanying loss of face and self respect. He would now cease to be the breadwinner and provider for his family, and in his mind would not be worthy to be the head of his family. He would have tried to maintain standards, but his weakness and dependence on others would have been hard to bear. Being unable 'to mend t'fire' was clearly a very deep loss and blow to morale.

In common with many people who grieve, when Albert could no longer deny his symptoms and became more aware that he was becoming chronically ill, he became angry and sought to attach blame for his condition. He had always been strong and so, he argued, if his body was weak now it must be because something had weakened it. The only cause that made sense to him was working for the Coal Board. It was clear cut to Albert so he further resented the fact that the Medical Board would not support his claim for compensation, and he felt cheated. In chronic illnesses the question of compensation, which is primarily for loss of earnings, is always an emotive one. If the compensation is not forthcoming, or is felt to be in-adequate, the patient and the family will not only feel a financial loss. They will also feel a loss of satisfaction in not seeing some form of retribution against those believed to be responsible for the disability. Receiving compensation can, in some instances, go a long way towards softening the blow and making the loss a little easier to bear. However, most would agree that no money can adequately compensate for the loss of a life in an accident, or for a life severely disabled by injury.

Before Albert became too disabled to get to the Miners' Institute for his pint he cut himself off, for financial reasons. His pride would not let him go there since he was unable to buy a drink for his mates. Rather than accept 'charity' he stayed at home, thus cutting himself off from the companionship he had cherished so much during his working life. Bit by bit he could see his life, and all that he had relied upon, being lost as a result of his illness and his reaction to it. In the words of Tennyson, Albert had to learn

> Tho' much is taken, much abides;
> and tho' we are not now that
> strength which in old days moved earth and Heaven;
> that which we are, we are.

Albert and his wife would need much support and 'listening to' in the months ahead.

Asthma

Asthma, in common with chronic bronchitis, can become a disabling condition. The patient may become demoralized if the attacks become frequent. If there are repeated attacks in rapid succession which exhaust the patient (status asthmaticus) admission to hospital may be necessary. The loss experienced by such patients will clearly be related to the age, sex and status of the person, but for the working person or the mother of a family

similar losses may be experienced to those described in relation
to chronic bronchitis.

The child patient may lose the opportunity to join in activities
with friends, which may also limit the choice of friends. There
may also be loss of schooling at certain periods of the year.
Knowing that one is 'marked out' can also lead to feelings of
stigmatization and retreat into illness as a means of gaining
attention. Over-protection of children can lead to feelings of
frustration because they think that their freedom is being cur-
tailed more than is necessary. A vicious circle can be set up with
the child resenting the parents' over-protectiveness and wanting
to rebel. The parents' anxiety may trigger off an asthma attack
and thus justify the parents in their over-protectiveness. Part of
the anxiety for the parents is their own fear and feeling of
inadequacy to help the child during an attack, together with a
measure of unresolved grief for the 'normal child' they seem to
have lost. A similar reaction can occur if the child has a disabling
heart condition.

An added problem in an illness like asthma, or chronic
bronchitis, is that there can be periods of remission. During
these periods the patient will feel much better and begin to talk
of going back to normal working now 'that there is nothing
wrong with me'. In many cases this works very well and during
a remission the whole situation can improve enormously. If a
realistic understanding of the illness has not been reached there
can be great resentment if another acute episode should occur.
Rather than being a period of denial, the time of remission
should become one of growth when the person attends to
building up their general health so that they may better cope
with any subsequent attacks. The grief process is often open-
ended since each acute episode serves to throw the patient back
into earlier grief reactions.

One of the main factors in the care of such patients is
supportive care to encourage them to persevere and co-operate
in treatment, whether it is drug therapy or physiotherapy. The
child or adult needs to acquire a knowledge of the nature of the

illness, warning symptoms, causes and the treatment to use when an attack is coming on. Such measures help to give confidence, reduce anxiety, and can serve to reduce the number of losses which the patient may subsequently experience.

Disseminated (Multiple) Sclerosis

Disseminated sclerosis (D.S.) is a disease in which degeneration occurs in the myelin sheath of some of the nerve fibres of the brain and spinal cord. The cause of the disease is, as yet, unknown and there is also no known cure. Usually the disease manifests itself in early adulthood with various transitory symptoms which vary in accordance with where the lesions or plaques occur. A typical patient would be young, lively, in previously excellent health and who goes to the doctor because of a suddenly developed neurological problem. For example:

A unilateral loss of vision together with pain in the eye, or misty or double vision. The optic nerve is frequently one of the first to be affected, but the symptoms usually disappear quite quickly.
Sensations of numbness and tingling in a limb, often an arm.
Dragging of one foot, clumsiness or staggering. Stubbing the toe on the pavement.
Weakened control of the bladder, with urgency of micturition and slight incontinence.[1]

In those cases where the disease progresses more nerve fibres are affected, the disabilities increase and the patient then becomes more and more helpless. However, it may be many years before this stage is reached and, irrespective of the initial symptoms, improvement or remission is usual, although further relapses must be expected. The duration of the disease has been known

[1] For further clinical details see Matthews & Miller (1976) p. 270.

to range from 2 to 20 years from the time of onset. Death usually results from pneumonia or chronic urinary infection. The tendency to spontaneous improvement is a remarkable feature of the early stages of the disease and can make diagnosis, and acceptance of diagnosis, difficult for all concerned. Some of the early symptoms may be passed off as being due to causes other than D.S. and this can be a source of embarrassment, or anger, or relief to the patient. A young man, who was seen to stagger and to have slurred speech one afternoon at work, was accused of having too much to drink at lunchtime. He had had a pint of beer, but nobody knew he had D.S. because he had kept it quiet in case he lost his job. A young woman, whose mother had died six months earlier, suddenly developed blurred vision and then partial blindness. She was given a diagnosis of 'hysteria' occasioned by grief. The fact that her sight returned as suddenly as it went was taken as proof of the correctness of the diagnosis.

In some patients the disease runs a chronic course from the beginning and the patient goes progressively downhill. For others, more favourably, there are successive severe episodes, with rapid resolution, speedy recovery and intervening periods without serious disability, perhaps for the rest of their life.

John first developed symptoms of D.S. at the age of 22 years. He found that he couldn't see out of his left eye and it was painful when he tried to look sideways. He was referred to a neurologist, but the symptoms cleared up before his appointment and so, as he did not like hospitals, he cancelled the appointment.

No further symptoms developed for about three years. Then he found that he was becoming unsteady on his feet. He began to lose confidence in going out as people would stare at him and make comments as he walked along. He found it was worse at the end of the day if he got tired. He seemed able to mask it at work but at weekends he would not go out unless it was with his wife and she could take his arm. This time he kept his appointment to see the neurologist. Several visits later the possibility of D.S. was discussed with John and his wife, and he was advised to change his job. He worked as a caster, which entailed carrying ladels of hot metal to the mould, and this was felt to be unsafe. John could see that he might lose his job and dreaded the loss of earnings and status as bread winner. He thanked the doctor for the advice, but decided privately to keep quiet about his illness at present, especially since they had a mortgage.

John and Anne had planned to start a family, but John was adamant that they should wait until his future was more settled. His wife found it hard to believe that he might have D.S. and wished to go ahead and start their family. She had always wanted children and this was a loss that she was not willing to accept. Eventually they agreed to wait another year and then review their situation. At this time John became moody and irritable and their marriage went through a very difficult period. John also became very depressed. One day the shop foreman talked to John about his slowness and that he didn't seem to be concentrating on his work as he used to, and at times was 'downright awkward'. After a heated exchange of words, John admitted his disability and contrary to his expectation did not receive the sack, but was offered the lighter job of 'checker'. On the basis that any job was better than none, he accepted.

A few months later, John agreed to use a walking stick. He was not happy about it but he found it saved a lot of explanations since people did not expect him to walk at their pace. He disliked the term 'disabled' and the prospect of a wheelchair appalled him and made him determined to keep going as long as possible. To keep going he needed to continue to use his car and he agreed to register as disabled so that he could have his car adapted for him to drive.

A year later John went into remission and his condition began to improve. He dispensed with his stick, applied for promotion, and told his wife it was about time they started a family! His remission has lasted four years and they now have a three-year-old son and are expecting another child. John is starting to say that he has been cured and refuses to listen if anyone mentions the possibility of a relapse. Whilst hope is a very important part of the care of patients with D.S., John and Anne will need a great deal of support if a relapse does occur.

No two people will experience the disease in the same way since the course it will follow, and the way it will present, may vary greatly from one person to another. While it is, therefore, difficult to generalize about the experience of loss for patients with D.S., certain problems do seem to be shared by many, and John and Anne's experience is not unusual.

The loss of previous good health can be difficult to accept and can lead the patient to deny any serious illness in the early stages. As the disease progresses and more symptoms manifest themselves there develops a growing awareness that 'all is not well'. This in turn leads to various forms of loss whose significance varies from person to person. The loss of function and independence can be very frustrating. Often the brain is functioning at a faster rate than the body and this can cause great irritation, anger and depression.

Because of the need to avoid fatigue and infection the patient has to learn new limitations and precautions. This does not imply developing into a hypochondriac or accepting inactivity at an early stage. It is important that the patient be encouraged to lead as active and independent a life as possible, in order to maintain morale.

Remaining in regular employment is an important part of this. In the early stages this may not be too difficult, depending upon the symptoms and the understanding of colleagues or workmates. The fear that one may lose one's job, and all that goes with it regarding money, status and independence, is a big factor in the morale of the patient, as shown in John's case.

The presence of urinary symptoms can also lead to embarrassment and a loss of dignity and self worth, which can make it difficult for the person to work if it means going to the toilet frequently. Some people could take advantage of this and it could lead to accusations that the person was avoiding work. Once again understanding colleagues can do much to help, if they know the reason why!

For the housewife and mother, the ability to care for her family is important and, to preserve this, many adaptations may be necessary in the home and special aids may be required. The local branch of the *Multiple Sclerosis Society* can be a great help in informing the person as to what help is available, as well as offering support in other ways to the family. Some people, however, do not wish to meet or have contact with other sufferers. John, who we discussed earlier, would not attend the Society's meetings since he didn't wish to meet people who might be worse off than himself, since he felt that he would be looking at himself in the future and this was too threatening. He also realized that such encounters would make it more difficult for him to deny that he had multiple sclerosis. He therefore denied himself an important source of emotional and social support at a crisis point in his life. It will probably be several years before he comes to terms with the disease sufficiently to accept help from other sufferers.

To be designated as 'disabled' can be an important change in status which seems to emphasize the loss of capability and self-esteem for many. The preservation of the person's morale, often in the face of increasing disability, is a major problem. The traditional 'euphoria' often helps the doctor, patient and family to cope, but one should not assume that this precludes depression since a reactive depression is quite common, and suicide is not unknown. One patient described how she sometimes became exhausted and felt a burden and how, on one such occasion, she planned her suicide in such a way as to cause the minimum of upset to her friends and relatives. However, following a rest and a cup of coffee she had felt less depressed and had shelved the plan. The sense of loneliness and of being a burden to others is a common reaction to loss in chronic illness, and there are parallels with the bereaved who sometimes experience a feeling of uselessness, that there is no point in going on with life.

There is one other aspect of loss which should be considered and which applies to other conditions as well. It is the loss of a sense of future and of security which is brought about by the cycle of *remission—relapse—remission*. This can lead to a sense of hopelessness if the periods of remission become shorter and the time between them lengthens. If a new drug or diet is being tried and the condition improves the patient will be hopeful of some lasting benefit. If this improvement has really been due to the start of treatment coinciding with a remission, there will be a great let-down if and when a relapse occurs. The maintenance of hope and as high a level of activity as possible seem to be important factors in minimizing the experience of loss for sufferers from disseminated sclerosis.

The parallel of adjustment to this illness with bereavement has been shown very clearly in a very helpful article by a young doctor who has suffered with the disease for several years. He writes:

I have now accepted the disease to a greater extent and no longer feel either depressed or angry about it. It has been like a long drawn-out bereavement, and I have had to come to terms with loss of health and ability and also to establish a new identity.[1]

The Epilepsies

A group of neurological disorders which can lead to the sufferer and family experiencing varying degrees of loss are the epilepsies. Once a diagnosis of epilepsy has been made the ordinary way of life can be destroyed because of the fears and prejudices of other people. In spite of attempts to educate the general public about epilepsy the condition is still surrounded by many myths and old wives' tales based on lack of understanding and experience. In Great Britain it is estimated that there are about 300 000 known sufferers[2] who experience difficulty because of the attitudes of others when they seek to compete in society and to develop the skills and abilities that they have. With medication, however, many epileptics are capable of functioning as

[1] Burnfield (1977) p. 436.   [2] Burden & Schurr (1976) p. xi.

well as many other people providing they are given a chance.

An epileptic seizure or fit is a transient disorder of cerebral function which is due to a sudden, brief and excessive electrical discharge of cerebral neurones. It frequently leads to convulsive movements which may be accompanied by loss of consciousness and loss of control over the bladder and the bowels. Over half the people who suffer from epilepsy had their first fit before the age of 20 years.

Symptomatic epilepsy is a term applied to fits due to localized structural damage to the brain or to generalized metabolic disorders which disturb cerebral function.

Idiopathic epilepsy is the term used when the precipitating factor is unknown and fits occur at intervals without any known organic lesion; abnormal electrical discharges in the brain being demonstrable by encephalography. Idiopathic epilepsy commonly manifests itself in childhood. Attacks may either take the form of *grand mal* (characterized by convulsive movements involving the whole body, unconsciousness and often incontinence) or *petit mal* (where there are brief lapses of consciousness but no convulsions).[1]

Some people make light of the illness and cope with it so well that others may not know that they have epilepsy. For others the seizures can be catastrophic and they may feel very lonely in suffering an illness which others do not seem to understand. It is difficult to accept that the uncertainties of epilepsy, the disturbance created by the attacks, and their unpredictable nature, will not have some effect on the individual's attitudes and way of life.

One of the early losses, resulting from the diagnosis of epilepsy in a child, is that experienced by the parents. For them there can be a sense of failure, guilt and shame, which is often coupled with lost hopes and dreams for their child. They may imagine a very bleak future for their child and anticipate difficulty in employment, in education, in marital prospects, and a fear of

[1] Passmore & Robson (1975) p. 34. 159 ff.

what will happen to the child when the parents die. This can lead to a very profound shock and grief reaction in many parents, which may be alleviated as they learn more about the nature and management of the condition.

Many of the losses experienced by the school child who has epilepsy are similar to those described in connection with the child who has asthma.[1] Being marked out as someone different can lead to various social barriers and a sense of not belonging. For the teacher of the child there are problems about whether allowances should be made in respect of performance, discipline and activities. Closely related to these is the question of responsibility if an epileptic child has an accident and the fears of this happening. Should the child, for example, be excluded from the gymnasium, the swimming pool, the cookery class and the metalwork class? The advice of the parents and the school health service is clearly important, but there can be no simple and universally applicable answers, for each child will be affected in different ways. The less restrictions the better for this clearly helps to reduce the social losses that can occur. These become more important as the child becomes older.

The school leaver faces the problem of employment. If the young person is very able, and can offer a skill which can offset the disability, then an employer may be more ready to offer a job. Unlike blindness, which is readily recognized, epilepsy does not always elicit understanding from employers or other employees. Several people have described their conflict at interview. The interview for a job is going very well and then someone asks a question about general health. If the epilepsy is reasonably controlled should one mention it or will it immediately end your chances and create a barrier. Those who have had such experiences often lose their confidence in the face of many rejections. It has to be acknowledged that certain tasks may not be suitable or safe for some epileptic people, but this can become an excuse for excluding them from certain firms. The

[1] See p. 92.

Disablement Resettlement Officer can sometimes help in easing some of the anxieties of employers and employees as well as helping to create a more helpful attitude towards the epileptic person. It is interesting to note that recent research has indicated that people who are bored, frustrated and depressed by their social difficulties become more prone to fits and that there is much truth in the phrase 'the best treatment for epilepsy is work.'[1]

Personality changes are frequently observed in the long term and are usually the result of social stigma, economic difficulties, recurrent cerebral hypoxia and the inability to cope with the losses that have been experienced. Many epileptics tend to become rigid, suspicious and demanding. Sometimes there is frank mental illness or mental deterioration with the patient becoming emotionally unstable. This may follow a period when the patient has had a large number of fits in quick succession.

It is important to assist the patient to lead as normal a life as possible and to create a clear understanding of the nature and control of the condition. Overprotection and unnecessary restrictions only serve to increase the sense of loss and resultant grief, which can become more disabling than the fits themselves.

Diseases of the Connective Tissue

The three most prevalent diseases of the connective tissue are osteoarthritis, degenerative disc disease and rheumatoid arthritis. These cause great suffering and disability to many people but, while they may last for many decades, they seldom threaten life acutely. Rheumatic complaints are second only to bronchitis as a cause of loss of working time in Great Britain, and rheumatism and arthritis have been described as the diseases which 'kill the fewest but cripple the most'.[2]

Rheumatoid arthritis is a very common crippling disease of

[1] Passmore & Robson (1975) p. 34. 55. [2] *Ibid.* p. 25,1.

the connective tissue which occurs in the 20 to 45 year age group. The onset is often insidious and the acute stage may subside, leaving some residual change. It can recur later, in the more severe cases, to render the patient increasingly disabled. Osteo-arthritis, by contrast, is confined to the joints but the disabling effect of the disease is very similar.

The reactions of the patient and the losses experienced are very similar to those already described in connection with other chronic and progressively disabling conditions. If the approach to the patient is a positive one, to encourage activity and the continuation of the treatment offered, the patient may be enabled to remain active and independent for a considerable time. If this does not happen and the patient is not well motivated he or she may become depressed, bedridden or chairbound with little interest in life and no hope for the future.

Cardiac Failure

Cardiac failure occurs when the diseased heart is unable to maintain a cardiac output adequate for the needs of the body. The heart fails because it is required to meet an increased mechanical load, or because of disease which interferes with the filling of the heart, or because the performance of the heart muscle is impaired.

If heart failure occurs during the natural course of hypertensive or ischaemic heart disease the prognosis without treatment is poor. However, treatment can greatly prolong the life of those with heart failure, whether such treatment is by medical or surgical means. One of the results of cardiac failure is the need for the patient to regulate his or her life to within the limits of the cardiac reserve, to avoid strenuous exertion and to modify the diet. If this can be achieved, many patients are able to retain a reasonably active life style within these limits. Therefore the extent of the resultant loss will depend upon the degree of cardiac failure and the age and social circumstances of the patient.

Many patients may be fit enough to remain in normal employment and so their illness may not lead to any economic or social loss, unless the condition deteriorates. Their friends and relatives, who know about their condition, may regard and treat them as invalids, and this can be a source of great irritation if they are fairly symptom free. On the other hand, some patients can 'use' their condition as a means of opting out of their normal life routine. Fear of aggravating the condition may lead the patient to impose restrictions on himself or herself which may not physically be necessary. This applies to other conditions, such as asthma, as well as cardiac failure. One example of this is in connection with the patient's sexual relationship. Sometimes a patient will think that he or she should cease from intercourse completely and may not discuss this with anyone. It can become a source of frustration in the relationship between husband and wife and this frustration can be displaced in other directions. Sometimes against the doctor who it is thought is responsible for the condition by virtue of making the diagnosis. The fear of an acute attack of the disease can also lead to impotence in some instances where sexual relationships continue. This is one area of patient care that is often avoided and the patient is frequently left to sort it out himself. The general practitioner is often in a better position to discuss this with the patient by virtue of his relationship with the family. It also needs to be borne in mind that some of the antihypertensive drugs can cause impotence (such as methyldopa and guanethidine) as well as depression in some patients.[1] One great loss for the woman who has cardiac failure can be the need to avoid a pregnancy. If the couple have no children and are unable to adopt, this can be a cause of great sorrow. If the woman should become pregnant a recommendation that the pregnancy should be terminated may also add to the distress.

The heart is still considered, by many, to be the centre of emotional life and that if anything is wrong with it, it is much

---

[1] *British National Formulary* (1974–6) p. 50 ff.

more serious than with any other organ. In offering support to patients with heart failure there is always the danger of iatrogenic distress (that is, distress induced by doctor/nurse/chaplain/family). Having a life assurance policy refused or being told of the need to live a 'very restricted' life can have a devastating effect on the patient. A positive approach to the patient and family, with encouragement to lead as normal a life as possible, can go a long way towards relieving some of the anxiety created by the term 'heart failure', and the losses that could follow.

The 'Stroke' Patient

Another medical condition which leads to a profound shock and sense of loss is that usually referred to as a 'stroke' or a cerebrovascular accident.

A stroke frequently happens to elderly people and occurs suddenly, leaving the person very disabled. Commonly the patient develops hemiplegia with weakness to one side of the body and there may be additional impairment of speech, sensation, intellect or vision. The event may happen suddenly during sleep, or while at work, or while performing some energetic task at home.

The outlook for such a patient will depend upon the cause of the stroke, the age and general health of the patient, the site and size of the brain lesion, whether there is loss of consciousness or other symptoms, and the family situation and support. Not all such patients will be admitted to hospital and a large proportion of them will be cared for at home by the general practitioner and the community nursing service. In a general practice of 2500 persons it is estimated that there are likely to be 5 new stroke patients per year, and a total of 15 to 20. In areas where the proportion of old people is higher this figure will be correspondingly higher.[1]

[1] Passmore & Robson (1975) p. 34.81.

In a bereavement, the initial shock protects the bereaved from a full realization of what has happened and the implications of the event as regards their future. However, the person gradually becomes more aware and begins to perceive, and react to, the various losses that have occurred. The same response and sequence of events can be seen with patients who are recovering from a stroke. Elderly people are often less resilient and dislike change, therefore the enforced change that follows a stroke can be hard for them to accept. It is a great shock to wake up and find that you are unable to move a limb, or to feel someone's touch on your arm or leg, or to find that you cannot speak. The fear that one might be dying is often not far from one's mind. As one lady remarked later:

I lay in bed thinking, 'Why am I dead on one side? Is this what death is like, dying in little bits? I know what I'm saying but why doesn't anyone understand me?' I was not sure at that time whether I would live or die and when people did not seem to respond to my words, although I thought I was talking clearly, I wondered if I was already dead. I was very frightened.

One of the first losses to be experienced is that of function, with the loss of the use of a limb, or speech, or control of the bladder. Closely associated with this is a loss of identity because the patient may dissociate from the person who is being described by the doctor as having various disabilities. The use of the patient's name is, therefore, important (as opposed to 'gran', 'pop' or 'ducks', however kindly such terms may be used) in order to re-establish identity and to increase the person's sense of worth. In the early days of treatment, especially if in hospital, there can be great activity with many investigations, drugs and physiotherapy. This concentrated attention helps the patient to feel that, whatever his present disability, he will soon be better because of this concentrated effort. During the first few weeks, the person may deny the extent of the illness and make light of the disability. In so doing he or she may overcompensate and hinder the rehabilitative process by ignoring medical advice because 'I don't need all that medicine, or to do all those exercises, because it's not so bad in my case and will correct itself.' Sometimes the patient may refuse to do exercises because these remind him or her of the limitations and so conflict with the person's self-image. This self-image is usually of someone who is healthy but who happens to have a *temporary* illness.

After the first few weeks of usually active treatment, the progress being made may slow down. The patient may then become depressed and believe that this means that they will never get any better and will not achieve a complete recovery. The person may focus only on what has been lost and be unable to acknowledge that they still have some ability left in the rest of their body. This leads the person to see their world in terms of 'a useless leg' and to have no regard for the fact that they have their sight, speech, and use of the other limbs. The mourning may be postponed by dwelling on the past and the ability they used to have. The present, in effect, holds nothing good enough to make it worthwhile giving up this image of themselves as they were.

The patient who is mentally alert, and imaginative, may react differently. He or she may well see what is ahead of them if progress does not continue and this can lead to conflict with those who are seeking to help. There may be complaints that not enough is being done, that the progress is too slow. 'I'm not getting enough walking' or 'Why can't I see the speech therapist more often?' The patient's natural impatience and frustration can lead to anger against the physiotherapist, the doctor or the family, but in many instances it can be used creatively as a drive towards independence. The increase in emotional lability which frequently accompanies a stroke can also complicate the picture.

Loss of independence is a source of great frustration for many and may lead to regression or resentment of help. The previous personality and character will clearly be important in determining the attitudes displayed and the extent of the recovery. Some patients will regress and display a childlike dependence which is especially true of people who, before their illness, were demanding. The person may lie back in bed and feel that it is up to others to get him or her better. As a chaplain I sometimes meet people who will not co-operate in their treatment. They lie back and pray 'God make me better', and then refuse to do what the physiotherapist asks them to because 'it's too difficult'. They seem to believe that God will sort it all out for them without any active contribution from them. Yet this is quite contrary to biblical teaching, where the person healed frequently had to *do something* specific as a part of the healing process—as his or her contribution. In the account of the healing of the 10 lepers[1] we read how Jesus sent them to show themselves to the priests to be pronounced clean. It was *as they went* that they were cleansed. They had their part to play and they were to be active participants and not passive recipients of healing.

Sometimes it is the relatives who may wish to keep the patient in a state of dependency. A wife, for example, in the initial stages of the illness, may like having her husband dependent upon her since this may satisfy her own need to be needed. Being unable to wash, shave, dress, feed and go to the toilet can be very demoralizing. While the patient may enjoy the attention and being waited upon in the early stages, the 'novelty' soon wears off and becomes a source of discontent. As in the case of the child with asthma, an over-protective attitude serves to increase the loss of independence, and thus lead to further resentment.

Many relatives are very ready to support and care for the disabled member of their family, whether at home or in hospital. However, for other families the admission of the elderly stroke patient can be a means of their being relieved of the burden of looking after the person, and they may not be too pleased when the patient begins to improve and may return home. This under-

[1] *St Luke's Gospel* 17, *v*. 11–19.

lines the importance of involving the family from the beginning in the care of the patient, whether at home or in hospital ward.[1] Relatives either wish to be part of the rehabilitative team or they come to be a patient alongside the patient! If their support cannot be obtained and sustained there is a danger that the patient will ultimately lose his or her place in the family because the family feel overwhelmed in the face of the patient's disabilities.

Once the patient has been discharged from hospital the patient will usually set about organizing the house and will have many new things to achieve each day. The same will apply if the patient has been nursed at home, because once mobility is achieved the patient will want to put his or her own stamp on the alterations that people have made to 'my' home while 'I was out of action'. Depending upon the circumstances various people may also call to make alterations to fittings in the home to aid the patient. This new wave of activity helps in the transition from a state of dependence to one of independence, (almost a *rite de passage*).

Within a short while this activity ceases and is frequently followed by further attacks of frustration, anger, hostility and depression which can all add up to a considerable loss of confidence. The patient may again begin to feel that, compared with his or her former self, he or she is now very inferior and not capable of achieving much. This can be a very difficult time for all who are involved and the patient will need much reassurance and persuasion to continue.

Each stroke patient is different from every other one, and the losses experienced will vary in number and in the patient's reaction to them. Although the recovery may be slow it can at times be quite remarkable, especially if one has been able to obtain the co-operation of the family from the start.[2] Optimism,

[1] See Keywood (1977) p. 66, on the teaching of relatives and maintaining their health.
[2] Carter (1968) Ch. 10.

based on a realistic appraisal of the patient's condition, at an early stage is seen to be an important factor in the successful rehabilitation of the patient.

Losses that May Lead to Illness

Mention should be made briefly of some of the instances where the illness seems to be caused by the loss rather than following on from it. The death of someone is the obvious example, but equally, divorce or redundancy can precipitate illness, especially a psychiatric illness.

Several G.P.s have commented to me that they have seen an increasing number of people in their surgeries with affective disorders, which seem to result from the effects of economic loss or social loss. One doctor described what he termed 'redundancy neurosis'. This affected mainly young or middle-aged people who had been made redundant or were unable to find employment. Their feelings of loss of status, self-respect and earning power had led to a depressive illness.[1] Some of these patients were well qualified academically and several, such as teachers, had received a professional training. When applying for jobs they had found themselves too highly qualified and their skills in many ways were a disability. They resented what they termed the 'dole stigma' and, together with the loss of a sense of purpose, this led to depression. Many such patients respond well to antidepressant therapy but some patients may overdose with drugs or alcohol, and there is always a danger of drug dependence or suicide.

Although such losses do not occur initially within the medical setting it is perhaps relevant to keep in mind the fact that, for some people, they can be the precursor of illness.

---

[1] On the difficulty of using terms such as 'reactive' and 'endogenous', see Passmore & Robson (1975) p. 35.49.

Conclusion

Patients who suffer from chronic illnesses experience several losses which often include the loss of independence, usefulness and purpose. The problems of employment for the young chronic sick can also be a source of stress together with the resultant change of status when a person is designated as 'disabled', which may lead to their no longer being socially acceptable. Since many chronic illnesses are not curable, those who care for the patient may also experience frustration and a sense of failure.

A positive and supportive approach to such patients, with continuing encouragement, can lead to their adopting a reasonably active lifestyle within the limits imposed by their illness. The extent to which this takes place is related to the nature of the illness, the age, the previous personality and the patient's ability to cope, as well as the support that he or she receives. The involvement and close co-operation between members of other disciplines, and the family, in the rehabilitation and ongoing care of the patient is very important.

References and Further Reading

British National Formulary (1974–6) London: British Medical Association.

Burden, G. & Schurr, P. H. (1976) *Understanding Epilepsy.* London: Crosby Lockwood Staples.

Burnfield, A. (1977) Multiple sclerosis: A doctor's personal experience. *Br. med. J., i,* 435–6.

Carter, A. B. (1968) *All About Strokes.* London: Thomas Nelson.

Chapman, C. M. (1977) *Medical Nursing.* London: Baillière Tindall.

Darling, V. & Thorpe, M. (1975) *Ophthalmic Nursing.* London: Baillière Tindall.

Eardley, A. (1977) The sick role and its relevance to doctors and patients. *Practitioner*, *219*, 385–90.

Keywood, O. (1977) *Nursing in the Community*. London: Baillière Tindall.

Matthews, W. B. & Miller, H. (1976) *Diseases of the Nervous System*. 2nd ed. Oxford: Blackwell Scientific.

Passmore, R. & Robson, J. S. (1975) *A Companion to Medical Studies*, Vol. 3. Oxford: Blackwell Scientific.

Perks, J. (1975) Nursing a blind patient. *Nursing Times*, October 30, pp. 1728–9.

Part Three
Cultural Factors and Grief

7   *Cultural Influences*

A culture may be defined as the way of living adopted by the people in a particular group. Every society will develop a particular set of arrangements to solve the problems of the members of that society. These arrangements form part of that society's culture and may be described as the *how* and *what* of social interaction. Different societies will develop different patterns and people's relationships with these cultural patterns are not static.

To some extent man is moulded in his behaviour by his culture, but he is also able to alter that culture by his action and to bring about change. Thus we find that some people will *conform* to the cultural patterns, others will act as culture *carriers* in teaching them to others, some will *manipulate* the culture to advance their own interests, and others will adopt a role of *creator* by challenging the status quo and bringing about innovation. Newly acquired knowledge may either be assimilated into the culture or rejected. This is especially true of modern medicine which may coexist alongside older and traditional concepts of illness, health and treatment, and the people of one culture may seek to transfer their attitudes and expectations onto the people of another culture. Doctors, nurses, social workers and clergy may therefore transfer from their cultural background various expectations of how people will, or should, behave in particular crises such as illness or grief. Society has certain expectations about what warrants grief and how much grief is appropriate. If a widow grieves for many months after the death of her spouse this is acceptable, although there may be pressure to get 'back to normal' quickly in some communities. If, however, a person grieves for many months over the death of a budgerigar this is not so acceptable, and people may regard the 'mourner' as foolish.[1]

The culture carriers will be looked to for ways in which the person may act out their grief and to find what behaviour is acceptable.[2] But people will grieve for what is important *to them* and for those they love, regardless of the yardstick which society may use to measure the appropriateness of the reaction. Losses have a very personal meaning to the individual who experiences them. Thus one woman who has a breast removed may be quite grief stricken because of the importance of the breast in her image of herself. Another woman may not be so distressed because she has not attached such great importance to her breasts.

In times of stress a person will utilize his own culturally acquired methods of coping which may seem inappropriate, or strange, to people of another culture. Following the Aberfan disaster it was observed that the expression of grief by the fathers was delayed for some time. Trying to get the fathers to express their grief sooner would have run contrary to their cultural patterns in that many of the families were so structured as to only permit the grieving role to a certain number at a time. Therefore, the husband waited for his wife and children to resolve their grief before expressing his own.[3] In this way there was always one member of the family who remained 'strong' and able to cope while the others coped with their grief. To people from outside the fathers must have seemed very 'hard'.

All societies have forms of ritual which are built into their culture and performed with traditional ceremony. Most rituals provide an acceptable way for an individual to act in a disturbing

[1] Keddie (1977) p. 21.   [2] Wilson (1975) p. 101.   [3] Miller (1974) p. 90.

situation. They are often group activities, or are performed by one individual on behalf of the group. Most of the major world religions have developed appropriate rituals in connection with many of the critical events of life. In the Christian Church, for example, there are services for 'Thanksgiving after childbirth', baptism, marriage, visitation of the sick and burial.

A group's understanding of health, sickness, life and death, and especially accidental death, is embedded in a complex of beliefs about man's relationship to the world in which he lives, to his fellow men, and to the supernatural powers which seem to govern the universe. It is not surprising, therefore, that many cultures express the belief that sickness is a punishment for not observing religious requirements. For the most part rituals have a protective function, but they can also be the means of effecting cleansing and healing.

The extent to which a ritual is found meaningful can influence the way in which some people cope with their bereavement. It is interesting to note that rituals have a power and a dignity which can affect even the most sceptical and that they can become real landmarks in a person's life. Used in an unimaginative way they can also appear to be completely irrelevant and to have nothing to say to the person in crisis. This sometimes leads people to dispense with ritual. One of the problems with that is that if people are then rushed to 'get back to normal' they may feel that grief is something abnormal and unacceptable. The person can then be at a loss to know how to express the turmoil felt inside.

Many forms of mourning ritual are designed to remove pollution, and to bring together and reintegrate the living group that has lost a member, and if possible to protect them from future ills. In some areas of Africa the living relations join together for the successive stages of mourning, and the 'gap' caused by the death is closed by another member of the kin group assuming the responsibilities of the deceased. Some cultures (such as the Chinese) have professional mourners who will show others how to act and what to do. The ritual therefore provides a means by which unpractised people can participate, communicate, and have a means of coping with feelings of helplessness and guilt.

In some parts of Wales and Northern England, clergy may be asked to conduct 'prayers in the house', before the funeral service in Church, Crematorium or Burial Chapel. Usually the coffin is in the front room, sometimes opened, and the family stand around it. Through the short scripture readings and prayers relatives and friends may be helped to say what they may find difficult to express by way of condolence to the mourners. The physical presence of the friends and relatives can also be a source of comfort. The service also acts in some sense as a means of cleansing, or exorcising, the house after a death, and this cleansing process continues after the funeral in the form of the wake.

When writing about the Irish wake-culture, Grainger describes how it can have a cathartic effect, releasing people from the need to conform to the usual standards of 'good behaviour' and therefore act as 'rites of passage'.

The wake itself signifies a return to chaos, a release from the restraints of normal 'good behaviour' and propriety, a real cultural disintegration, analagous to the dissolution of the deceased's earthly identity and authority. The final requiem and burial are thus islanded in time, and attain a kind of post-cathartic solemnity, the deliberation of grief is acknowledged and accepted, the calm of all passion spent. Such post-liminal rites act as monuments to whatever has gone before; not only the death of people or animals, but of institutions, epochs, stages of growth, even attitudes of mind. They are real 'rites of passage'.[1]

The rites and customs associated with funerals would seem to have a threefold purpose: psychological—by giving a frame-

[1] Grainger (1974) p. 120.

work for the expression of grief; theological or philosophical—which may help the mourner to make some sense and meaning out of what he or she is experiencing; sociological—the comfort derived from knowing that others are willing to share the experience and give support, and ultimately to receive you back into the normal life of the group. If this threefold purpose is to be achieved, and the needs of the mourner are to be met, then funeral rites must be adaptive, meaningful and a means of enabling the person to move in a healthy, reintegrating direction.

It helps to know something about the cultural background of those we care for in the community, but is equally relevant when the patient is admitted to hospital. If a patient in hospital suffers a bereavement he or she will have the added problem of trying to cope with their grief in an 'alien setting'. The patient can be greatly helped in this if staff understand some of the needs of the patient, which he or she may find difficult to express. In the case of the patient who is dying, this can mean that the patient can be enabled *to die his own death*, and not someone else's culturally imposed upon him or her.

Sometimes there can be a conflict between the pattern of ward life and the person's cultural expectations and norms, which can lead to a sense of lost identity and dignity. This can occur for someone from our own culture, but the feeling can be heightened for a patient from another culture since the various cultural and religious needs may not be recognized and met. It may also be difficult for the patient to understand and accept some aspects of ward life and medical routine.

Therefore, from both sides of the bed, *it can help if one understands*.

Summary

Within any society there will be arrangements which enable the members of that society to solve their problems. Some of the people in that society will act as either carriers, conformers, manipulators or creators of these arrangements or cultural patterns.

Ritual has an important part to play in this process by enabling the person who has suffered a loss to move in a healthy and a reintegrating direction. If the ritual is to be relevant it must meet needs at three levels: the psychological—by giving a framework for the expression of grief; the theological or philosophical—by which the person seeks to make some sense and meaning out of what is experienced; the sociological—through sharing the experience with others and being reaccepted into the society.

References and Further Reading

Grainger, R. (1974) *The Language of the Rite*. London: Darton, Longman & Todd.

Keddie, K. M. G. (1977) Pathological mourning after the death of a domestic pet. *Br. J. Psychiat.*, *131*, 21–5.

Miller, J. (1974) *Aberfan—A Disaster and Its Aftermath*. London: Constable.

Mitford, J. (1963) *The American Way of Death*. Harmondsworth: Penguin.

Read, M. (1966) *Culture, Health and Disease*. London: Tavistock Publications.

Wilson, M. (1975) *Health is for People*. London: Darton, Longman & Todd.

It Helps to Understand

In this chapter we shall look at some of the attitudes and beliefs of a *selection* of the ethnic groups in Great Britain to such topics as dying, last offices of the dead, autopsy, burial, cremation and grief. It must be stated at the outset, however, that not all members of a particular religious or ethnic group will be equally strict adherents to the various beliefs and practices of that group. It is always advisable, therefore, to seek the guidance of the patient and the family concerning any special needs and wishes. This is especially important in relation to terminal care and the admission to hospital of non-English-speaking patients.

The Christian

At the heart of the Christian faith is the person of Jesus Christ, whom Christians believe to have been both human and divine. They accept His teachings and try to follow them. The historical roots of the Faith lie in Judaism and the belief that man was created by God in the 'image and likeness of Him' and that man shares in the creative nature of God. In the act of creation, man was given 'freewill' which allowed him to choose whether or not he would follow God's ways. By various acts of rebellion, both individual and corporate, the relationship between man and God was spoilt, and these events are recorded in the Old Testament of the Bible. The New Testament contains the teachings and events in the life of Jesus, together with the development and application of that teaching in the life of the early Church.

Christians believe that is is through the death of Jesus Christ that mankind has been reconciled to God. They also believe that by Christ's resurrection He overcame death and evil, and that He gives new life to those who believe and trust in Him. This new life extends beyond the grave and may be experienced by the believer when he becomes a Christian. In most instances this is marked by baptism with water in the 'name of the Father, and of the Son, and of the Holy Spirit', and the person affirms his belief in Jesus Christ as the Son of God and in the statement of belief known as the Creed. The person also promises that he will, by God's help, live out a Christian way of life, study the scriptures, pray regularly, and share in the corporate life of the Church and its ministry of the Word and Sacraments. If baptism has taken place in infancy it is followed later in life by a ceremony (Confirmation or Membership) whereby the person makes the promises his or her own. Although the individual has to discipline himself or herself to live out this new way of life, he does not do so unaided. He receives the guidance and strength of the Holy Spirit of God, the support of other Christians and the strength made available through the Holy Communion, whereby the person may come into close contact with Jesus through the sharing together of the bread and wine blessed by the priest or officiating minister.

The main themes of the teaching of Jesus are: God's rule is more important than anything else in life; God cares for all; God's true children are those who love as He loves; God's love is present in a very special way in the person of Jesus Christ. The Christian who has accepted Christ is, therefore, exhorted to live out the commandment 'You shall love the Lord your God with all your heart, and with all your strength, and with all your mind; and your neighbour as yourself'.[1] The nature of

---

[1] *St Luke's Gospel* 10, *v*. 27.

this love is also important, as it is to be a 'selfless' love—'even as I have loved you'.[1] This simple statement can become very complicated when one looks at the ways in which different groups of Christians have interpreted and applied it, and it is not possible in the space of a few pages to cover all ways in which the different groups express their faith.[2]

Attitudes to suffering and death

Within the Christian tradition various groups (denominations) tend to lay emphasis on different aspects. There are also many who have not thought out in any depth the implications of their faith for some aspects of their life. Therefore, one might best illustrate some of the Christian attitudes to suffering by two examples of an understanding of suffering within the Christian tradition.

One morning I received a phone call from the surgical registrar to ask whether, as chaplain, I would see one of his patients who was refusing surgery. The patient was a 35-year-old West Indian lady. She had given her religion as 'Christian' when she had been admitted to hospital for investigation. The surgeon had explained that she probably had a tumour but she flatly refused to have an operation. When I visited her she handed me her Bible which contained a 'bible tract'. The leaflet explained that cancer was the devil in disguise and that the surgeon's knife would cause the devil to spread until he took over her body and her life. I asked if, as a Christian, she felt that she should fight evil and the devil. She agreed. Then I suggested to her that she should allow God to eradicate the evil within her through the hands of the surgeon. She thought for a while and then said, 'All right, as long as I know that the surgeon is a Christian!' I contacted the surgeon who visited the lady and

---

[1] *St John's Gospel* 13, *v*. 34.
[2] See Brown (1975) p. 252 for suggestions for further reading.

assured her that he was a practising Christian, and that he would be starting his day by attending Mass. I saw the lady on her way to theatre, with a big smile on her face. Four years later she was still doing well. The religious belief of this lady clearly affected her attitude to her illness and the prospect of surgery. Whatever views one might hold oneself, for her, sickness equalled evil and the cause was the devil, the time to widen her understanding came later.

By contrast, a 50-year-old man with a cancer of the tongue explained to me that he knew he was terminally ill and that he had 'wrestled with God' as he tried to understand why. He went on to say that after a long while he realized that the world was not perfect and that sickness was part of that imperfection and did not show any discrimination between people. It was not God's fault that he was ill and he had eventually asked himself the question 'What does God want me to make of this situation?' He began to be less depressed and started to take a more positive approach to each day, so that his life, whether long or short, would be a full one. As he approached death he said that he had made his peace with God and believed that he would soon be healed (made whole). By this he meant that, although his body would die and there might be no physical healing, he would soon be with God and become a 'whole person' *at-one* with himself and with God. He said, 'I am no longer preparing for death, but for real Life'. There were two biblical passages which gave him great comfort and support at this time:

Jesus said: 'I am the resurrection and the life; he who believes in me, though he die, yet shall he live, and whoever lives and believes in me shall never die.'[1]

For I am sure that neither death, nor life, nor angels, nor principalities, nor things present, nor things to come, nor powers, nor height, nor

[1] *St John's Gospel* 11, *v.* 25, 26.

depth, nor anything else in all creation, will be able to separate us from the love of God in Christ Jesus our Lord.[1]

The ministry of the Word and the Sacraments, as well as the prayers of others, had been very important in the attainment of peace of mind for him and his family.

To some people, therefore, sickness and death become symbols of disorder in the world which are a result of man's freewill being exercised—and not a part of the original creation. Thus they become understandable in terms of human interdependence rather than because of cause and effect between a particular sin causing a particular death or disease; although this does sometimes happen. For many Christians, illness is consequential rather than punitive and it is often unmerited, but capable of being used by the believer as an opportunity for growth, personally, interpersonally and spiritually. Healing is seen by many Christians as a process of restoration of the wholeness of the personality and as a means of reconciliation between man and God. Death may be part of this process. Prayer is seen as turning towards God and opening to Him so that the Holy Spirit may be able to work in the person's life. This may take place silently, verbally, individually or corporately.

In many churches there is a growing practice of healing services. The services usually include an act of faith and of penitence, bible reading, prayer, the 'laying on of hands', and thanksgiving. Those present may also receive Holy Communion. Groups may emphasize different aspects but generally all agree that one is placing oneself before God and asking for strength to cope with the particular disability. One is also asking God to grant 'wholeness', or at-one-ness, which may or may not include physical healing. The act of laying hands on the person's head is a means of conferring God's blessing and of assuring the person of the love, support and prayers of those present. The 'laying on of hands' may sometimes be followed

[1] *Romans* 8 *v*. 38, 39.

by anointing the person with holy oil.

Different Christian denominations may emphasize different aspects of the Christian faith. However, all agree that in ministering to the dying one should endeavour to preserve as peaceful an atmosphere as possible. The patient should be given every support and opportunity to prepare for death in the way he or she wishes, and that after death the body of that person should be treated with respect and dignity, and the usual 'last offices' performed. All the Christian churches now accept cremation as an alternative to burial, which may or may not be preceded by a service at the Church usually attended.

The Roman Catholic church would normally wish a priest to attend a dying patient so that the Sacrament of the Sick might be administered. This was formally associated with 'last rites' but now the Sacrament is administered to people who may not necessarily be terminally ill and is intended to aid their attainment of true health, and not just as a preparation for death. Usually the person will, if able to, make an act of confession, receive absolution, holy communion and the anointing with oil.[1] This service can give great comfort to the relatives as well as the patient and the new emphasis (as in the Anglican church) avoids making the patient too apprehensive, since the Sacrament may be administered more than once. If the patient is a baby there may be a request that the child should be baptised. This usually only happens if the child's life is endangered in any way since baptism normally takes place in church. If a priest is not available any person may baptise the child by pouring water over the child's head and, using the child's name, saying, 'I baptise you in the Name of the Father, and of the Son, and of the Holy Spirit.' The priest should be informed as soon as possible. The parents' permission should always be obtained before baptism takes place, especially since some Christians do not agree with the baptism of babies.

The Free Church or Nonconformist ministers are the least

[1] *Epistle of James* 5, *v.* 14–15.

ritualistic in their ministry. The Anglican church shows a wide variance in that some clergy may place great emphasis on the ministry of the Word whilst others lay greater emphasis on the ministry of the Sacrament, but not implying that these are mutually exclusive. It is best to consult with the patient and family as to whether they wish to see a clergyman of their own particular denomination since some will benefit from the presence and actions of a priest, whereas others may become anxious because of their own ill-formed ideas and beliefs. However, even the most anxious, if approached in a sensitive way, may gain some ease and peace of mind through conversation with a minister.

The Jewish Community

The Jewish faith is based on the *Torah*, which comprises the first five books of the Old Testament, being God's law as given to Moses and the Israelite people over 3000 years ago. The other principal holy book is the *Talmud*, which is an explanation and application of the written law. These contain the basic rules of life for a Jew which he or she will try to conform to, with the help of the Rabbi or teacher. The extent to which these precepts are adhered to will depend upon whether the person is an orthodox, a reformed or a liberal Jew. Circumcision is practised and is usually performed on the eighth day.

When a Jewish patient is dying great comfort is derived from saying or listening to *Psalms* 23, 103 and 139 and the use of a 'confessional' which acts as a *rite de passage* to another phase of existence. The Rabbi will usually visit if specifically asked to by the patient. If possible a practising Jew would wish to say or hear the words, 'Hear, O Israel, the Lord our God is one'[1] at the time of death. For the practising Jew there is a structure which provides a realistic approach to death, but with the minimum of anxiety, as also happens in some of the other

[1] *Deuteronomy* 5, *v.* 4.

major religions. The family would usually wish to be present, but the dilemma of communicating the severity of the illness to the patient is just as real for the Jewish community as for any other.

After the patient has died, dignity and perfection at all times is stressed. Therefore, while a non-Jewish nurse may perform the last offices it is advisable to use disposable gloves so that there is no direct contact with the deceased. The requirement of perfection and freedom from mutilation means that permission will usually not be given for autopsy, unless there is a medico-legal requirement. Occasionally a request has been made for the return of an amputated limb so that the deceased may be buried whole.

This requirement for perfection and freedom from mutilation can also affect the reaction of the patient to mutilating operations which may not readily be agreed to unless absolutely necessary. Some of the Hebrew congregations in this country have people who will come and prepare the body for burial, but only at the specific request of the family and not as a routine referral from the hospital or community services. Burial usually takes place within 24 hours of death. If a Jew dies on the Sabbath (Saturday) then the body will be left until the Sabbath is ended. However, someone will stay with the body and mourn until the burial, and a candle will be burnt in the home. Cremation is not acceptable as a rule, though some modern Jews do favour it.

The grief work commences by being present with the dying person, but because of the close knit family life and community life it suffices if a member of the community is there, if the next of kin is unable to be. Observing the death helps to preserve a sense of reality since it is not so easy to later deny the death. This links in with what was said earlier in relation to helping parents accept the reality of a stillbirth. Judaism also provides a structure for the burial and the mourning, to guide the mourner and enable the resolution of grief to be achieved.

After the person has died the mourner, therefore, is not

shielded but expected to take full responsibility for the funeral arrangements and is freed from religious observances at this time so that he or she can devote time to this task. The funeral is usually very simple with no flowers and the avoidance of ostentation. *Kriyah*, the tearing of the clothes, is a visible and dramatic symbol of the internal feeling of being torn by grief. When the mourner looks at the garment later it also has a cathartic effect and leads to further expression of grief. During the burial service the person is encouraged to openly express grief, especially during the time of the eulogy. Later, when the coffin has been lowered into the ground, those present in order of kinship cast earth into the grave and do not leave until the grave has been filled. This is in contrast to many other funerals where the mourners are steered away from the graveside as soon as the commital has taken place.

After the burial the community turns its attention to the bereaved, and on the return from the cemetery a meal will have been prepared as an expression of their care. So far the mourner will have been allowed to withdraw in his or her own pain and grief. In some groups the mourner is consoled at inappropriate times and rushed through the mourning period. In the Jewish community there is a sequence of events with set periods for the various events, during the ensuing year. First there are three days for deep grief. Then seven days of mourning during which condolence calls are made. The visitor's main role being to *listen* and not to talk. This follows the funeral and is in keeping with the saying in the *Talmud*, 'Don't console the mourner in the presence of his dead'. During these seven days the bereaved person who is in hospital would greatly appreciate having free access to visitors if possible, especially if he or she has been unable to attend the funeral. Then follows a period of 30 days of gradual readjustment and eleven months of remembrance and healing. On the anniversary a candle is often lit in the home and special prayers said in the synagogue.[1] At the end

[1] Gordon (1975) p. 44.

of this year it is expected that the mourner will be well integrated back into the life of the community.

The Muslim Community

Their faith

It is usual to speak of Muslims, and to call their faith Islam, whose prophet is Muhammed (not Muhammedans). The holy book is the Qur'an and their holy day is Friday. A *practising* Muslim has a set of systematic rules to order his life, known as the Five Pillars of Islam, but there is much flexibility, especially when the person is sick, elderly or weak.

Food. Pork and alcoholic drinks are forbidden. Strict Muslims would not touch or serve pork or pork products. Other types of meat, as eaten by Christians, are acceptable provided they are ritually killed. In many cases a Kosher diet, as prepared for a Jewish patient, is acceptable to the Muslim patient in hospital. Some Muslims will abstain from meat completely and keep to a vegetarian diet.

Childbirth. The newborn baby, soon after its birth, 'listens' to the Call to Prayer. The shaving of the baby's head at birth is common and is a symbolic act to take away the 'uncleanliness' of childbirth, as well as to help the hair grow in greater profusion. Many Asian mothers apply black cosmetic to the eyelids of their babies. Their own preparations often contain lead and mercury and so they are gradually being introduced to Western eye makeup. However, this practice is dying out in many areas.

Circumcision is obligatory for the male Muslim child. There is no fixed age and this can be done at any time before eight years, although it usually takes place on the seventh day. It can be synchronized with the separation of the umbilical cord seven or eight days after birth. Circumcision is not done under the N.H.S., but often a Muslim doctor will perform this act (as will a Jewish doctor) as a service to a member of his own community.

Stillbirth can sometimes lead to a supression of grief. The mother may feel very sorrowful at the death of the child, but she may also feel that 'it shall be as Allah decrees' and that to express any grief is to express a lack of faith in Allah. Therefore, she may try very hard to 'shrug it off' and to seem to accept what has happened. The term 'Muslim' means 'one who surrenders to God', and so she may wish to surrender herself to God and accept what has happened as His will. If the child was a male child this may create added tension, especially if there are no other male children, since she may forsee difficulties in her marriage if she is not able to produce a male child. This can also affect the attitude of a Muslim lady who is recommended to have a hysterectomy, or not to have any more children for medical reasons. Permanent sterilization is not acceptable, neither is abortion unless there is a choice between the life of the baby and the mother. The general principle in the Qur'an is that one should weigh up the good and the bad of any situation and act accordingly, therefore, apart from sterilization, birth control becomes a matter for decision by the couple themselves. The need for a male child still remains a very significant factor in reaching a decision.

Some Muslim women are very reluctant to undress and allow themselves to be examined. If a woman doctor is not available it is not a 'sin', according to their faith, for a woman patient to expose any part of her body that a doctor needs to examine. In antenatal care it may, of course, be harmful if a woman will not be examined and there have been instances where Pakistani ladies have died rather than be examined. This would seem to be more a matter of social education among people of very orthodox rural background, since a Muslim is urged to seek the best possible medical treatment if ill.

Death and dying

When a person is about to die it is the practice in general that someone recites the Qur'anic verses, especially Ch. 36, entitled *Yaa Seen*, for bringing peace to the soul. Then at the moment of death, 'Surely we are Allah's and to Him we shall surely return'. Since the dead body is washed as part of the funeral rites it is not usual for the hospital to wash the body. The head of the deceased is turned towards the right shoulder so that the person may be buried facing Mecca. The use of disposable gloves allows last offices to proceed, with the removal of drainage tubes and other equipment, without risk of defiling the deceased. The body is straightened, the eyes and mouth closed and the big toes are fastened together.

Members of the family will attend to the washing, and this is performed by someone of the same sex as the deceased, repeating words from the Qur'an as they do so. After the washing the body is usually clothed in three pieces of white unsown cloth for a man, and five pieces for a woman. The outer part of the shroud is the largest and covers the entire body. No coffin is used for burial and the person is interred in a niche in the side of the grave so that earth does not touch the body when the grave is being filled in.

Muslims are vigorously opposed to cremation, which they associate with uncleanliness. They are also very opposed to autopsy, even if requested for medicolegal reasons.

If a Muslim patient is bereaved while in hospital then, as with the Jewish patient, unrestricted visiting is greatly appreciated. Many Asian people with their close knit families find it difficult to accept our Western concept of restricted visiting hours, especially if they are newly arrived in this country and have come from rural areas of India or Pakistan.

A Muslim burial. The head of the corpse is turned towards Mecca.
(Reproduced by permission of the Director of the India Office Library and
Records).

The Hindu Community

Their faith

Unlike Christianity or Islam, Hinduism has no single prophet or Messiah, no formal creed or central authority such as the Church. Worship is conducted in the home and if the family attends a Temple there is no set form of worship and each family follows its own pattern. The ancient Aryan writings (the *Vedas*), together with the *Upanishads* and the *Bhagavad Gita*, form the basis of much Hindu thought and date back to around 2500 B.C. However, the *Guru* (Teacher/Guide) occupies a very important place as the one who steers the *individual* Hindu on his path through life.

Hinduism is very complicated but the *basic* beliefs are:

1. The transmigration of the soul with indefinite reincarnation, so that your next life depends on your behaviour in the present life. The escape from the cycle of birth–death–rebirth lies in the dissolution of all desires. This idea is shared with Buddhism.
2. The division of society into social classes (caste system) which determine which tasks could be undertaken by which caste in order to avoid contamination—such as the handling of a dead body. The caste system is now illegal in India, but reflections of it can still be seen sometimes.
3. The worship of a complex system of gods and goddesses who are, in effect, subsiduary aspects of the 'One Supreme Being' (*Param Atma*). The three main divinities are *Brahma* (the creator), *Shiva* (the destroyer) and *Vishnu* (the preserver).

Certain people are also revered by Hindus: parents by their children, husbands and wives revere each other, teachers and professional people by pupils, and priests and ascetics are revered by all. There is also a great reverence for all forms of life. Termination of a pregnancy would cause deep distress to a Hindu patient.

Sickness and admission to hospital

Hindus usually abstain from eating beef and veal and their derivatives. Many are vegetarian and abstain from alcohol. When admitted to hospital they may, in common with many Asian people, find undressing embarrassing. They may also prefer to take a shower rather than a bath, since many Asian people find it distasteful 'to sit in your own dirty water'. Cleanliness is very important. The left hand is usually used for the unclean tasks, such as personal toilet, and the right hand for eating and performing clean tasks. A person, therefore, may experience great loss of dignity because of a divergence from the laws of conduct relating to hygiene, social behaviour and spirituality. He or she may also fear a loss of status when rejoining the Hindu community after discharge from hospital. A deeper sense of loss is experienced if the patient feels that the experience of being in hospital has affected his existence in the succession of lives after death, and thus hindered his attainment of Nirvana.[1] For this reason the Hindu (in common with patients of other faiths) should be allowed to practise his religion while he is in hospital.

When a male Hindu is initiated and takes his vows he has a 'sacred thread' placed over his shoulder. This thread is to be worn for life and care should be taken not to remove it unless vitally necessary, and with the patient's prior permission.

Hinduism has an age-old cosmology which combines many features of modern astronomy. One consequence of this is the belief that the results of human actions are influenced by patterns formed by the heavenly bodies. Thus there are propitious times for having important things done. A Hindu may, therefore, refuse a long-awaited operation if he finds that the date offered to him by the surgeon is unpropitious. However, it must be stressed that many Hindus are very liberal in their attitudes and may conform to standard hospital routine without much difficulty or distress.

[1] The loss of self by fusion with ultimate being.

A Hindu cremation. Both Hindus and Sikhs cremate the dead. (Reproduced by permission of the Director of the India Office Library and Records)

Religious rites associated with birth and death

At the first sign of pregnancy the child will be blessed within the mother. On the tenth day after birth, the child is named by a priest. At the onset of puberty the adolescent undergoes the 'sacred thread' ceremony and makes his vows as someone 'twice born'.

Family planning can be accepted by Hindus with complete moral and intellectual freedom, and it is therefore a matter for individual couples to decide for themselves.

A dying person may derive great comfort from hearing or reading the words of the *Bhagavad Gita*, especially Chapters 2, 8 and 15. A Hindu priest may be called if the patient or family wish, and he may give his blessing and tie a thread around the neck or the wrist of the patient. This signifies the blessing and should not be removed. Similarly, the 'sacred thread' should be left on a male patient. Prolonged vigils by the bedside are thought to be unseemly and distressing and the family will probably go home to pray for the person. The Hindu would usually prefer to die at home, often on the floor, so that he can be near to Mother Earth. Since there is no ritual washing of the body after death there is no reason why last offices cannot proceed as with any other patient

It is important, where possible, that the eldest son is informed of the imminent death of the father, since he has responsibility for the funeral arrangements, and in India he is the one who sets light to the funeral pyre, and attends to the ancestral ceremonies. The compelling drive for a Hindu man to have a surviving son is partly explained by this rite, which has great religious significance. The ashes are later scattered on water, if possible the Ganges which is a sacred river. An autopsy is not forbidden for a Hindu, but the idea of autopsy is distasteful, and much persuasion is needed.

In this country cremation is the norm although occasionally Hindus will ask for burial, especially in the case of children.

The Sikh

In many ways their faith combines the *essence* of both the Hindu and Muslim religious outlook at their best. The founder of the Sikh religion was Guru Nanak (born 1469) who taught that everyone should have direct communication with God, and that no one should have special privileges by reason of birth, wealth, religion, race or sex. The way of salvation was through a good life of kindness to others and concern for family and society.

There were only ten gurus and the last one formed a new brotherhood (the Khalsa) which was a military body. They were all baptised with sweetened holy water, and he then established the five marks which all baptised Sikhs should wear:

Keshas   the uncut hair, though some in Britain have now shaved their beards and cut their hair.

Kanga   the comb, used to keep the hair in place as a bun on top (known as the 'top knot') A turban goes on top and a Sikh does not like it to be removed.

Kara   the steel bangle, worn by men and women on the right wrist to remind them of their obligations and of the unity of God.

Kirpan   the short sword, for defence and to symbolise dignity. Now often worn as a brooch or pin.

Kachcha   a pair of shorts as underwear, to remind of sexual discipline. A Sikh patient would find it offensive to have these shorts removed unless absolutely necessary. To avoid loss of dignity he may wish to shower with them on.

Birth and death

The Sikh place of worship is the Gurdwara, and it is here at birth that the Sikh child is named. The holy book (*Ad Granth*) is opened at random and the first word of the verse at the top left hand corner of the left page is used. Hence some Sikh boys and girls may have the same name. A few years later the rite of baptism is performed by five devout Sikh men who sprinkle nectar on the person, while he or she is exhorted to follow Sikhism. From then on the suffix of 'Singh' (Lion) is used for a Sikh boy and 'Kaur' (Princess) for a Sikh girl.

Sikh women are usually more outward-going than other Asian women, and more ready to enter into British society. They are not regarded by their menfolk as in any way inferior. Guru Nanak once said, 'How can women be regarded as inferior, when they give birth to the greatest men'. However, they still retain a great deal of modesty.

The Sikh and Hindu attitude to life and death contain many similarities, and both accept cremation and believe in reincarnation. Cremation takes place after the relatives have paid their respects and read the Sikh hymns over the dead body in the home. As with Hindus, there is no reason why last offices should not proceed as usual.

The emphasis in the Sikh life on good works, patience, hospitatility, and care for others often means that in times of sickness the Sikh will adapt well to being in hospital, and to co-operating with those who offer health care.

The Buddhist

I go for refuge to the Buddha
I go for refuge to the Dhamma (teaching)
I go for refuge to the Sangha (monks)

These are the words used by the devout Buddhist as he begins his meditation before an image of the Buddha. Buddhism arose against a background of Hinduism in the sixth century B.C. Buddha was formerly a Hindu prince whose eyes were opened to the problem of suffering, as a result of which he left his palace and family and devoted his life to finding the cause and answer to this problem. His answer lay in meditation which led him to the 'four noble truths' which are:

1. That existence is unhappiness.
2. That unhappiness is caused by selfishness and craving.
3. That desire can be destroyed.
4. That it can be destroyed by following the '*noble eightfold path*'. The steps of this path are *right desires*; *right speech*, plain and truthful; *right conduct*, including abstinence from immorality and taking of life in any form; *right livelihood*, harming no one; *right effort*, by persevering; *right awareness*, by knowledge of past, present and future; and lastly, *right contemplation* or meditation.
   The more someone acquires merit by following the Path in his chain of lives the sooner he will reach *Nirvana* where he loses his individuality by merging with the universal life.

Buddhism has spread to many parts of Asia and the Western world and the culture of the particular country affects the way in which some aspects of the 'way' are practised. Tibetan Buddhists, for example, insist strongly on cremation, while Chinese Buddhists lay great emphasis on the preservation of the body and prefer burial. This is more because of the Chinese culture than because they are followers of Buddha.

Many Buddhists would hold that modern medicine seeks to restore the patient to physical well-being and that in cases of chronic illness such relief may only be temporary. Buddha's main aim was also to treat 'ills' (*dukkha*) and to pay special attention to the conditioning of the mind to an acceptance of changing situations with serenity. 'Mind is the forerunner of all evil and good conditions: it is the chief; mindmade are all things.'

In Buddhist scriptures one finds four factors playing a significant role in maintaining the physiological process. If these four things are out of tune they will promote pathology, not health. They are: deeds occasioned by volitions (*Kamma*), mental disposition (*Citta*), atmospheric conditions (*Utu*), nutriments to feed body, senses and the rebirth process (*Ahara*). The root cause of the 'ills' which afflict mankind are the cravings and desires, and the eight-fold path is the only way to freedom.[1]

A practising Buddhist would, therefore, argue that while organic disorders will require medical treatment, the psychological sequelae can best be coped with by Buddhist meditations to relax the mind and body and to help the patient learn to see things in their true perspective. This in many cases should lead to a better therapeutic response as, for example, with patients suffering from hypertension. The achievements of physical and mental health are not to be ends in themselves, but means towards the higher goal of spiritual health. The Buddhist is attracted by the concepts of sacrifice, surrender and renunciation and would seek to transcend physical difficulties. This would be achieved by his own efforts. In contrast, the Christian would seek a similar goal but through acceptance of Jesus Christ and in the power of the Holy Spirit or God.

There is general agreement between the Hindu and the Buddhist that human life can have little meaning and efficacious action unless it is lived in full acceptance of the fact of the reality of death. People are instructed by Buddha not to make plans without first reckoning with death, which may strike at any time and is no respector of persons. Hence one should meditate on one's death while one is in health. A preparatory text for this meditation is *The Tibetan Book of the Dead* which may be compared with the nineteenth century Christian work of Jeremy Taylor, *Holy Living—Holy Dying*, which states that one's pattern of living affects one's pattern of dying: 'It is a great art to die well, and to be learnt by men in health'.

A terminally ill Buddhist patient would wish to maintain clarity of thought for as long as possible. Clear consciousness is regarded as crucial for the finest death and the patient may

[1] Soni (1976) p. 141.

not wish to receive pain-killing drugs unless absolutely necessary. In terms of 'loss' the Buddhist who is unable to achieve
this not only suffers a sense of loss in this life but it also means
a loss in his next life. Every effort should be made to provide
quietness for meditation, and to help the person achieve calm-
ness, hopefulness and joy. At the time of death there are no
specific rituals relating to the last offices and anyone may prepare
the body for cremation. Since it is believed that Buddha was
cremated, this method is usually used for the bodies of notable
people. Western Buddhists do not seem to attach any great
importance to the choice of method. The culture of the family
seems to be the deciding factor. As with the other groups in
society it is best to consult with the family, whenever possible, as
to any specific wishes and needs.

The Chinese

The religion of the Chinese people is usually a mixture of
Taoism, Confucionism, Buddhism and ancestral worship. Many
younger Chinese may have rejected the traditional beliefs or
may have become Christians or atheists. Many Chinese are
fatalistic and very practical about death. They believe that just
as there has to be a birth to mark the beginning of a life, so there
has to be a death to mark its end. Each person who is born
already has a destiny mapped out with a right time to die. Like
the Hindu, an operation may be refused if it coincides with an
unpropitious date.

When the person dies in hospital members of the family will
often visit the hospital to assist with the last offices, and may
wish to dress the body in new clothes ready for the journey to be
undertaken in the new life. A similar practice is found in some
branches of the Armenian and Russian Orthodox churches. The
emphasis on completeness may lead the family to refuse permission for an autopsy. At the time of the funeral there is an open

expression of grief and, if the family is very small, then professional mourners may be employed. Paper money is burnt at the
time of the funeral to provide the deceased with money to spend
in the next life.

It is believed that the spirit of the deceased is present at the
funeral together with other spirits, who may not all be good
ones. For this reason they use fire crackers to chase away the bad
spirits, and when the body is interred they turn their backs on
the coffin. The family of a terminally ill patient may ask for him
or her to be admitted into hospital to die, so that the spirit of
the person will not haunt the home afterwards. Conflict sometimes arises between the older Chinese people, who may wish
to observe the ancient customs, and the younger Chinese, who
may wish to dispense with them. If the family is Christian they
will often wish for a Christian burial service instead.

Humanism

'Man is the measure of all things' is the keynote in humanistic
philosophy, which believes that man himself can improve his
own conditions without supernatural aid, and indeed has a duty
to do so. A humanist has faith in man's intellect to bring knowledge and understanding into the world and to solve the moral
problems of how to use that knowledge. Respect for one's
fellow man, irrespective of class, colour or creed is fundamental
together with the moral principles of freedom, tolerance, justice
and happiness. The close relationship between mind and body
means it is inevitable, says the humanist, that when the body
ceases to exist at death the whole life of man is finished. Thus
there is no belief in immortality. In the words of Bertrand
Russell, 'I believe that when I die I shall rot, and nothing of my
ego will survive.'[1]

For the humanist death poses no great problem, though the

[1] Russell (1957) p. 43.

process of dying may do. Reconciling the 'dignity of man' with a long and painful terminal illness can raise difficult questions about the means of ending that life. Emphasis on the completion of a life, of having rendered valuable service to mankind, and the dignity of a human being all help the person to submit to the inevitable end. As mentioned in Chapter 3, the end of life for a Christian and for a humanist is often marked by dignity and courage. It is the last days of the person who is uncertain that are often most traumatic for all concerned.

The humanist emphasis on achievement in this life leads to a concentration of effort in the solving of problems of pain, sickness and death, which limit that level of achievement. However, this motivation to research and discovery need not be any less strong in other belief systems, such as Christianity, where the relief of suffering and a dignified death are held to be important.

Conclusion

The various religious beliefs and cultural patterns referred to all influence the thinking and practice of the dying patient and family. They serve to explain some of the wide range of reactions and requests that anyone caring for the terminally ill may meet, which can range from glad acceptance to petrifying fear. Not everyone will be an equally devout adherent of their religion or philosophy of life and many will not have thought out a clear religious, agnostic or atheistic position. The prime need in all cases is for privacy, quietness, comfort and free access to such religious ministration and help as the patient may desire. Above all, a sensitive attitude on the part of those caring for the sick person may be more helpful than scrupulous attention to the minutae of a particular religious ritual.

References and Further Reading

Bowker, J. (1975) *Problems of Suffering in Religions of the World.*
London: Cambridge University Press.

Brown, D. A. (1975) *A Guide to Religions.* London: S.P.C.K.

Gordon, A. (1975) The Jewish view of death: guidelines for
mourning. In *Death, The Final Stage of Growth.* ed. Kubler
Ross, E. Englewood Cliffs, N.J., U.S.A.: Prentice Hall.

Polson, C. J. & Marshall, T. K. (1975) *The Disposal of the Dead.*
London: English Universities Press.

Russell, B. (1975) *Why I am Not a Christian.* London: Allen and
Unwin.

Soni, R. L. (1976) Buddhism in relation to the profession of
medicine. In *Religion and Medicine III*, ed. Millard, D.
London: S.C.M. Press.

9   *Time is the Great Physician*

When one considers the wider meaning of the terms loss and grief one can see the necessity of allowing people more *time* to readjust to loss than might otherwise be allowed. Cultural expectations influence the time we allow people to grieve and what we consider to be appropriate occasions for grief. The time we allow for people to readjust is often related to the value *we* place on the lost object, person or function, and this may differ widely from the value the bereaved attaches to that which is lost. In the case of a young woman who has a miscarriage it may be assumed that, because she hardly knew she was pregnant, she will soon get over it and would be best advised to 'forget about it and try again fairly soon'. The young woman, however, may perceive the event differently and, if she and the staff are unable to share the way they perceive the event, the various needs will only be met by chance (see Chapter 4).

If the individual is to be supported before and after the loss is experienced, there needs to be a sensitive awareness of the value of the lost object to the person, and the implications for the person's life subsequently. This implies a relationship between the patient and staff which allows for listening; controlled involvement; and the sharing of realistic information, emotional responses and encouragement. This further implies a similar relationship between staff members if they are to gain any confidence in their ability to handle emotionally open communication, and to cope with their own feelings.

The concept of anticipatory guidance (see Chapter 2) provides one way of achieving this by mobilizing the person's strengths and defences beforehand so that one is able to meet a loss more constructively. The main features of anticipatory guidance are:

Realistic information. This allows the person to have a better idea of what he or she is likely to experience. This leads to the recognition of one's vulnerability and stimulates worrying. This information may be given verbally, or in leaflet form. Depending upon the nature of the loss being anticipated, the information given might also include the discussion of cosmetic aids, prostheses and rehabilitation, as well as the expected postoperative condition of the patient. The amount of information given, and the way in which it is given, will depend upon the patient, the form of loss, and the experience and skill of the person giving the information.

Reassurance. Anticipatory reactions often lead to feelings of helplessness, fears for the future and pessimism. Therefore the giving of realistic information needs to be backed up by reassurance of what help can *actually* be provided, without any false promises. Alerting the person to the reality of the impending loss must be balanced by realistic assurances of help and support.

Active participation. The other main feature of such guidance is the encouragement of the person to sort out his or her resources to cope before the loss occurs. There is always the danger that one can make the person feel so helpless that he or she will rely passively on others. This sometimes presents itself to me, as a chaplain, as the patient who prays 'God make me well', and then refuses to cough for the physiotherapist. If the patient's coping mechanism is not mobilized early enough and the patient adopts a passive role, there can be anger and bitterness against the family, doctor, nurse, or God for letting the loss happen.

It might be argued that a patient who is awaiting an operation would be best advised to spend the time preoperatively taking his or her mind off what is going to happen. This seems a very obvious truth, but it is not borne out by studies that have been made.[1] Most people who experience a loss seem to cope better if they are *enabled* to rehearse the unpleasant aspects of the experience and to stimulate their coping repertoire, rather than pretending the loss is not going to happen.

All this clearly takes time and people may feel, with all the other pressures that are on them, that they have not really got any spare time to devote to this form of preparation—even if they feel it is worthwhile. If we accept the wider meanings of the terms loss and grief, and the relevance of anticipatory guidance, then the time spent in this way should lead to a reduction in subsequent distress, and the need to spend more time treating abnormal grief reactions.

A sensitive awareness of the possible implications of loss and grief, and the willingness to listen, can go a long way towards helping the person who has suffered an important loss to grow from the experience and to move in the direction of health and a new sense of wholeness. Whatever else we may be able to offer to those in need, one very important gift is that of *time*. Time to listen and time to readjust; since, as Disraeli commented, 'time is the great physician'[2]

References and Further Reading

Disraeli, B. (1880) *Endymion*.
Janis, I. L. (1971) *Stress and Frustration*. New York: Harcourt Brace Jovanovich.

[1] Janis (1971) p. 95 ff.   [2] Disraeli (1880) vi, Ch. 9.

Appendices

Appendix 1   Discussion Topics

These discussion topics are offered as a means of relating the material in the book to ourselves, both personally and professionally. It is envisaged that these discussions will be interdisciplinary.

1. Consider the various forms of loss that you have experienced in your life time. How far do you think that you have been able to use these experiences to grow in understanding, or have they led to a stunting of growth in certain areas of your life? To what extent do you think these experiences affect how you relate to people you care for and who are experiencing or anticipating loss?

2. People sometimes find anger difficult to accept and attempt to suppress it, or to become defensive or to avoid the aggressive person. How can we use, creatively, the anger expressed by someone who is grieving?

3. What advantages and disadvantages can you see with the concept of anticipatory guidance? Can such guidance present problems if it becomes part of a wider educative programme, for example, by telling too much, too soon?

4. How feasible is the concept of 'emotionally open communication'? How might it be employed in your own work?

5. 'Distress can be almost like a contagious disease in that it raises feelings of anxiety in those involved with people in distress.' How far does this statement match your own experience and how can you cope with it?

6. In the event of a stillbirth, or the birth of an abnormal child do you think it helps to show the parents the child? What criteria would you use to help you decide which parents may or may not benefit from this?

7. What might be the advantages and disadvantages in giving leaflets to patients as a means of preparing them for surgical loss? What information should be given to patients admitted for mastectomy, the creation of a stoma or the amputation of a limb?

8. The society which stigmatizes the stoma patient, or the mutilated person, is frequently the same as that which 'expects' the medical profession to perform such operations to eradicate disease. How can such inconsistent attitudes be reconciled?

9. A male patient of 40 years of age, married with two children, develops chronic renal failure and is subsequently trained for home dialysis. What forms of loss might one expect to be experienced by the patient, the various members of the family, and those caring for him?

10. In caring for a patient with a chronic condition there may come a point when the emphasis in the approach to the patient moves from quantity to quality of life. How does

one assess quality? What conflicts might this give rise to and how does one accept the limitations of one's ability to cure?

11. What are *your* expectations of someone who has experienced the loss of an important object or person? To what extent should the patient, the family, yourself and the routine of hospital life adapt to each other's expectations?

12. Funeral rites and the 'wake' provide a ritual for people following the death of another person. Is it feasible to devise relevant, meaningful, rituals or 'rites of passage' for people who have experienced other forms of loss?

Appendix 2 *Useful Addresses*

Some useful addresses for guidance and support in Britain.

Association of Parents of Vaccine Damaged Children
   2 Church Street, Shipton-on-Stour, Warwickshire

Association for Spina Bifida and Hydrocephalus
   30 Devonshire Street, London, W1N 2EB

British Council for Rehabilitation of the Disabled
   Tavistock House (South), Tavistock Square, London, WC1H 0LB

British Epilepsy Association
   3–6 Alfred Place, London, WC1E 7ED

Central Council for the Disabled
   34 Eccleston Square, London, SW1V 1PE

Colostomy Welfare Group
   38 Eccleston Square (Second Floor), London, SW1V 1PB

Cruse (National Widows Organization)
   Cruse House, 126 Sheen Road, Richmond, Surrey

Cystic Fibrosis Research Trust
   5 Blyth Road, Bromley, Kent, BR1 3RS

Down's Babies Association
   Quinborne Centre, Ridgacre Road, Quinton, Birmingham, B32 2TW

General Welfare of the Blind
   8–22 Curtain Road, London, EC2

Ileostomy Association of Great Britain and Ireland
Drove Cottage, Fuzzy Drove, Kempshott, Basingstoke, RG22 5LU
Mastectomy Association of Great Britain
1 Coleworth Road, Croydon, CR0 7AD
MIND (National Association for Mental Health)
22 Harley Street, London, W1N 2ED
Multiple Sclerosis Society of Great Britain and Northern Ireland
4 Tachbrook Street, London, SW1V 1SJ
National Association for Mentally Handicapped Children
Pembridge Hall, Pembridge Square, London, W2 4EP
Parkinson's Disease Society
81 Queens Road, London, SW1 8NR
Royal National Institution for the Blind
224 Great Portland Street, London, W1N 6AA
Royal National Institute for the Deaf
105 Gower Street, London, WC1 6AH
Samaritans
Church of St Stephen's, Walbrook, London EC4
Society of Compassionate Friends (Help for Bereaved Parents)
The National Secretary, 8 Westfield Road, Rugby, Warwickshire
Spinal Injuries Association
24 Nutford Place, London, W1H 6AN
Urinary Conduit Association
33 Avondale Road, Edgley, Stockport

Bibliography

Bibliography

Ballinger, C. B. (1977) Psychiatric morbidity and the menopause: survey of a gynaecological out-patient clinic. *Br. J. Psychiat.*, *131*, 83–9.

Boore, J. R. P. (1977) Preoperative care of patients. *Nursing Times*, March 24, pp. 409–11.

Bowker, J. (1975) *Problems of Suffering in Religions of the World.* London: Cambridge University Press.

Bowlby, J. (1971) *Attachment and Loss.* Vol. 1, Attachment. Harmondsworth: Penguin.

Bowlby, J. & Parkes, C. M. (1970) Separation and Loss. In *The Child in His Family*, Vol. 1 of International Yearbook of Child Psychiatry and Allied Professions. ed. Anthony, E. J. & Koupernik, C. New York: John Wiley.

British National Formulary (1974–76) London: British Medical Association.

Brown, D. A. (1975) *A Guide to Religions.* London: S.P.C.K.

Burden, G. & Schurr, P. H. (1976) *Understanding Epilepsy.* London: Crosby Lockwood Staples.

Burnfield, A. (1977) Multiple sclerosis: a doctor's personal experience. *Br. med. J.*, *i*, 435–6.

Caplan, G. (1969) *An Approach to Community Mental Health.* London: Tavistock Publications.

Capra, L. G. (1972) *The Care of the Cancer Patient.* London: Heinemann Medical.

Carlson, C. E. (1970) *Behaviour Concepts and Nursing Intervention.* Philadelphia, U.S.A.: Lippincott.

Carter, A. B. (1968) *All About Strokes.* London: Thomas Nelson.

Chapman, C. M. (1977) *Medical Nursing.* London: Baillière Tindall.

Darling, V. & Thorpe, M. (1975) *Ophthalmic Nursing.* London: Baillière Tindall.

Department of Health and Social Security (1975) *Funerals for Stillborn Infants.* DS 211/75. London: HMSO.

Devlin, H. B., Plant, J. A. & Griffin, M. (1971) Aftermath of surgery for anorectal cancer. *Br. med. J., iii,* 413.

Devlin, H. B. (1973) Stoma care—the quality of life. *Stoma Care.* Queensborough: Abbott Laboratories.

Disraeli, B. (1880) *Endymion.*

Doak, N. (1976) We're a couple of swells. *She,* February, p. 40.

Eardley, A. (1977) The sick role and its relevance to doctors and patients. *Practitioner, 219,* 385–90.

Edwards, J. G. (1976) Psychiatric aspects of civilian disasters. *Br. med. J., i,* 944–7.

Engel, G. (1962) *Psychological Development in Health and Disease.* Philadelphia, U.S.A.: W. B. Saunders.

Fish, E. J. (1974) *Surgical Nursing.* London: Baillière Tindall.

Gath, A. (1977) The impact of an abnormal child upon parents. *Br. J. Psychiat., 130,* 405–10.

Goffman, E. (1968) *Stigma.* Harmondsworth: Penguin.

Goligher, J. C. (1975) *Surgery of the Anus, Rectum and Colon.* London: Baillière Tindall.

Gordon, A. (1975) The Jewish view of death: guidelines for mourning. In *Death, The Final Stage of Growth.* ed. Kubler Ross, E. Englewood Cliffs, N.J., U.S.A.: Prentice Hall.

Grainger, R. (1974) *The Language of the Rite.* London: Darton, Longman & Todd.

Hannam, C. (1975) *Parents and Mentally Handicapped Children.* Harmondsworth: Penguin.

Hill, S. (1974) *In the Springtime of the Year.* London: Hamish Hamilton.

Hinton, J. (1967) *Dying*. Harmondsworth: Penguin.

Hunter, D. J. S. (1974) Effects of hysterectomy. *Lancet, ii,* 1266.

Janis, I. L. (1958) Emotional inoculation: theory and research on effects of preparatory communications. In *Psychoanalysis and the Social Sciences*. New York: International Universities Press.

Janis, I. L. (1971) *Stress and Frustration*. New York: Harcourt Brace Jovanovich.

Jolly, H. (1976) Stillbirth—a new approach. *Nursing Mirror,* October 7, p. 4.

Jones, M. (1977) Mastectomy. *Nursing Times,* April 21, p. 559.

Keddie, K. M. G. (1977) Pathological mourning after the death of a domestic pet. *Br. J. Psychiat., 131,* 21–5.

Kessler, H. H. (1951) Psychological preparation of the amputee. *Ind. Med. Surg., 20,* 107–8.

Keywood, O. (1977) *Nursing in the Community*. London: Baillière Tindall.

Kitzinger, S. (1977) *Education and Counselling for Childbirth*. London: Baillière Tindall.

Kolb, L. C. (1954) *The Painful Phantom*. Springfield, Illinois, U.S.A.: C. C Thomas.

Kubler-Ross, E. (1970) *On Death and Dying*. London: Tavistock Publications.

Lewis, C. S. (1961) *A Grief Observed*. London: Faber and Faber.

Lewis, E. (1976) The management of stillbirth—coping with unreality. *Lancet, ii,* 620.

Lindemann, E. (1944) Symptomatology and management of acute grief. *Am. J. Psychiat., 101,* 141.

Maguire, P. & Hampson, M. (1976) The operation was successful but the patient wants to die ... *Wld Med.,* Nov. 3, pp. 35–7.

Mathers, J. (1970) The context of anxiety. In *Religion and Medicine, I.* ed. Melinsky, H. London: S.C.M. Press.

Matthews, W. B. & Miller, H. (1976) *Diseases of the Nervous System*. 2nd ed. Oxford: Blackwell Scientific.

May, R. (1969) *Love and Will*. London: Souvenir Press.

Menzies, I. (1960) A case study in the functioning of social systems as a defence against anxiety. *Hum. Relat., 13,* 95–121.

Miller, J. (1974) *Aberfan—A Disaster and Its Aftermath.* London: Constable.

Mitford, J. (1963) *The American Way of Death.* Harmondsworth: Penguin.

Letter—on stillbirth. (1976) *Nursing Mirror,* October 21, p. 44.

Oates, G. D. (1973) Colostomy and ileostomy. *Stoma Care.* Queensborough: Abbott Laboratories.

Parkes, C. M. (1973) Factors determining the persistence of phantom pain in the amputee. *J. psychosom. Res., 17,* 97–108.

Parkes, C. M. (1975) Psycho-social transitions: comparison between reactions to loss of a limb and loss of a spouse. *Br. J. Psychiat., 127,* 204–10.

Parkes, C. M. (1975) *Bereavement: Studies of Grief in Adult Life.* Harmondsworth: Penguin.

Passmore, R. & Robson, J. S. (1975) *A Companion to Medical Studies,* Vol. 3. Oxford: Blackwell Scientific.

Perks, J. (1975) Nursing a blind patient. *Nursing Times,* October 30, pp. 1728–9.

Pincus, L. (1976) *Death and the Family.* London: Faber and Faber.

Polson, C. J. & Marshall, T. K. (1975) *The Disposal of the Dead.* London: English Universities Press.

Read, M. (1966) *Culture, Health and Disease.* London: Tavistock Publications.

Richards, D. H. (1973) Depression after hysterectomy. *Lancet, ii,* 430.

Richards, D. H. (1974) A posthysterectomy syndrome. *Lancet, ii,* 983.

Robinson, N. & Swash, I. (1977) *Mastectomy. A Patient's Guide to Coping with Breast Cancer.* Wellingborough, Northants: Thorsons.

Russell, B. (1975) *Why I am Not a Christian.* London: Allen and Unwin.

Schilder, P. (1935) *The Image and Appearance of the Human Body.* London: Routledge & Kegan Paul.

Schoenberg, E. ed. (1970) *Loss and Grief.* New York, U.S.A.:

Columbia University Press.

Sellwood, R. A. (1974) Prognosis and rehabilitation of patients with cancer of the rectum and colon. *Stoma Surg. Rehabil.* Queensborough: Abbott Laboratories.

Shorter Oxford English Dictionary (1970) London: Oxford University Press.

Smith: Jo Ann Kelley (1977) *Free Fall.* London: S.P.C.K.

Soni, R. L. (1976) Buddhism in relation to the profession of medicine. In *Religion and Medicine III.* ed. Millard, D. London: S.C.M. Press.

Speck, P. W. (1970) Visiting in a psycho-geriatric ward. *Br. J. Psychiat., 117,* 93.

Speck, P. W. (1973) The hospital visitor. *Nursing Times,* July 5, p. 878.

Speck, P. W. (1976) East comes west. *Nursing Times,* April 29, p. 662.

Speck, P. W. (1976) The relative nuisance. In *Religion and Medicine III.* ed. Millard, D. London: S.C.M. Press.

Speck, P. W. (1978) Easing the pain and grief of stillbirth. *Nursing Mirror,* June 1, pp. 38–41.

Spraggon, E. M. (1975) *Urinary Diversion Stomas.* Edinburgh: Churchill Livingstone.

Symposium on Stoma Care (1976) *Nursing Times,* January 8.

Tew, B. J., Laurence, K. M., Payne, H. & Rawnsley, K. (1977) Marital stability following the birth of a child with spina bifida. *Br. J. Psychiat., 131,* 79–82.

Tillich, P. (1965) *The Courage to Be.* London: Fontana Library, Collins.

Wilson, M. (1975) *Health is for People.* London: Darton, Longman and Todd.

Wright, B. A. (1960) *Physical Disability—A Psychological Approach.* New York: Harper and Row.

Biblical Quotations and References

Deuteronomy 5, *v*. 4.
St Luke's Gospel 10, *v*. 27 and 17, *v*. 11–19.
St John's Gospel 11, *v*. 25–6; 13, *v*. 34; and 16, *v*. 21.
Romans 8, *v*. 38–9.
I Corinthians 15, *v*. 54.
James 5, *v*. 14–15.
Revelations 21, *v*. 4.

Index

Index

Figures in italics indicate illustrations

Hair (Sikh religion) 138
Healing
abnormal child 45
10 lepers 107
process of, role of self-help
107
services 125
spiritual purpose 125
Health, pride of elderly 89
Heart
centre of emotional life 103
failure 102
Hemiplegia, of stroke 104
Hindu faith 134
on suffering and death 137
Holy Living—Holy Dying
141
Home adaptations
in multiple sclerosis 96
in rehabilitation of stroke
108
Homosexual male, rectal in-
cisional surgery 65
Hope, for parents of abnormal
child 44
Hospital
arrangement of funerals 41
bereavement in 119, 129,
132
Hindu faith 135
Hostile reactions, in bereavement 9, 16
Human qualities, nursing staff
23
Humanism 143
Humour, adjustment to surgical loss 56
Husband's role, grief of miscarriage 35

Hypertension, cardiac failure in
102
Hypochondria of chronic illness 83
Hysterectomy 48
information leaflet on, Middlesex Hospital 50
Muslim 131

Iatrogenic stress, in heart failure
104
Identification
in marriage 17
staff with patient 27
with deceased 10, 16
Identity loss, in stroke 105
Ileostomy 65
Ileostomy Association 65
Illness
as punishment 117
symbol of disorder in world
125
Image of deceased 9
Impotence, in heart failure
103
Independence loss, in stroke
106
Infertility 43
Insecurity, of chronic illness
97
Intellect, impairment, after
stroke 104
Involvement 27
Ischaemic heart disease 102
Islam 130

Jesus Christ, teachings of 122